THE DEATH OF
CONTENT

AS
KING

HOW A DATA DEMOCRACY HAS
REVOLUTIONIZED MARKETING

JON HINDERLITER

TACTICAL 16
PUBLISHING

The Death of Content as King:
How a Data Democracy Has Revolutionized Marketing

First Edition
Because of the dynamic nature of the internet, any web address or links contained in this book may have changed since publication and may no longer be valid.
The views expressed in this work are solely those of the author and do not necessarily reflect the views of the publisher, and the publisher hereby disclaims any responsibility for them.

Published by Tactical 16, LLC
Monument, CO

ISBN: 978-1-943226-54-2 (paperback)

This book is dedicated to my fellow veterans,
who understand that freedom is not free.

CONTENTS

Chapter One: The King is Dead 1
   A Revolution in Binary 2
   The King that was Promised 4
   The Sun Never Sets on the Content Empire 7
   Content Marketing Regime 8
   No King Rules Forever 8
   The Rise of a Data Democracy 10

Chapter Two: Living in the Data Democracy 13
   If a Tree Falls in the Woods, Was Marketing Responsible? 15
   The 5 W's 17
   Form Follows Function 18
   The Struggle of the Old Guard 20
   No Such Thing as a Free Lunch 22
   The Value to Marketing 23

Chapter Three: A Platform by Any Other Name 25
   Pick a Color — Any Color 26
   Let Me Google That for You 28
   Et Tu, Google 29
   Everything is Connected 30
   Solve for Intent 33
   Brand vs. Non-Brand 36
   Actually, it's Both: the Journey and the Destination 39
   Search Ends with Intent in Mind 41

Chapter Four: It's a Social World After All 43
   Facebook Platform 44
   Move Fast and Break Things 47
   Stay Focused and Keep Shipping 49
   Hacker Way 51
   The Foolish Wait 55
   Our Work is Never Over 58

Chapter Five: The Everything You Didn't Know You
Needed Store 61
   The Everything Platform 62
   It's All About the Long Term 63
   Obsessing Over Customers 65
   The Infinite Looping Marketplace 67
   From A to Z to Threat 69

New and Improved Virtuous Cycle 74

"Alexa, Send Me an Easy Button" 75

If a Head is Cut Off, Two More Shall Take its Place 78

Chapter Six: Targeting the Consumer's Journey 79

Choose Your Own Adventure 82

Modern Consumer Decision-Making Journey 84

Retention Journey 90

Data Abhors a Vacuum 92

Chapter Seven: Personalization at Scale 95

Greeting Card Content 97

HELLO: My Name Is 98

Just Scale It 101

Moneyball Fandom 102

Who's Watching Who? 104

Chapter Eight: Building a Data Democracy 107

Starting a Data Revolution 109

VOTE Data Framework Model 110

Responsible Democracy 112

Greetings, Programs! 113

Do Hackers Dream of Electric Sheep? 116

If You Build It, They Will Come 117

Chapter Nine: Privacy in the Era of Data Democracy 121

Don't Be Creepy 124

Red Team 125

Facebook Under Siege 126

The Walled Garden Approach 128

This Is Why We Can't Have Nice Things 129

Chapter Ten: What's Next for the Data Democracy 133

The Content Wars 2: Streaming Edition 135

Good Morning Hal 136

There Can Only Be One 138

Worlds Built on Data 140

Author's Note 145

Acknowledgements 147

Notes 149

Bibliography 161

About the Author

About the Publisher

CHAPTER ONE

The King is Dead

My first job in marketing was writing content. For five years, I wrote copy every day for the first casino in Illinois, Argosy Casino Alton.[1] Every month it was my job to make sure the casino's direct mail, which included cash, food, and entertainment coupons, was in players' hands before the first of each month. If it wasn't, I was out of a job before the end of the day. The constant deadline pressure didn't bother me. I was getting a chance to make a living writing copy. Besides the direct mail, I updated the casino's website with more content, designed promotions, and generally helped the casino keep up with emerging trends in technology, like email marketing and smartphone apps.

As the months turned to years, I started to realize that the content I was writing didn't make any difference in player behavior. Of course, people were always going to come to the casino for gambling, live concerts, and food specials. But I thought it was my job to get people excited about what was happening each month. Still, the more time I spent talking with the casino's customers, I realized that it wasn't my content that was driving more or less business. Instead, it was the value of their direct mail coupons.

The turning point for me was when I was sent to the casino's corporate home office in Wyomissing, Pennsylvania for training on their customer relationship management (CRM) software. I wasn't directly responsible for the CRM system at the casino, but being technologically savvy, I was considered the preferred backup to the CRM marketing coordinator. It was in those training sessions that I began to understand where the real value in marketing resided. Not in written copy about elaborate promotions, upcoming concerts, or the newest slot machines, but rather the incredible amount of data the casino had about their players. The data was recorded by each player's reward cards, inserted into slot machines, and tracked at table games. From that data came an understanding of player visitation habits, which helped the casino turnabout one million dollars in cash coupons and rewards into over twenty million dollars in casino revenue each month. It was with data that the marketing team was able to achieve its goals for the casino, instead of content.

After I left the casino industry and pursued a deeper career in data-driven marketing, I realized that not everyone shared my awakening about the lack of value for content. The more time I spent around marketers, communicators, and public relations professionals picking up an assortment of buzzwords, jargon, and catch-phrases, a single phrase was being repeated ad nauseam: "Content is King." Even outside of marketing, this mantra had found believers in the news, entertainment, publishing, and other industries. All sought to both embrace the fast pace of technology changes while acting as knights of the old guard of media, given shiny new armor to prove its value in a changing world. For over two decades now, this mantra has been repeated countless times in articles, blogs, websites, books, conferences, and marketing agency mission statements; each dedicated to this singular school of thought. I repeatedly found myself having to prove that a revolution had arrived in marketing with data rising over content. That content as king was dead.

A Revolution in Binary

This book examines the fundamental paradigm shift that has occurred in marketing, communications, and media with the death of content and the rise of data. It's undeniable that data has changed the nature of modern business, and professionals at all levels are expected to understand the meaning behind every metric in this informational era. And yet, content continues to be viewed as the dominant force. Meanwhile, every observable, measurable, and actionable marketing decision can be made using data almost directly from the consumer. This data from the internet and the devices that bridge the gap into the physical world now act as the voice of the people. Data hasn't simply become the new king, but it serves as the foundation of a new data democracy.

In order to understand the revolution that has taken place, the downfall of content must also be analyzed for its overabundance and uselessness. For marketers, life inside this new data democracy shows the difference between what content cannot do and what data can, since consumer actions occur at any given moment. This is dependent on learning what types of data can be trusted, from what sources, and how to model that connection with consumer intent. For consumers, how their data acts like a vote gives them an advantage in how they are treated similarly to real-world democracy.

As majorities rule in a democracy, so do a few organizations that use the data they collect to both improve the experience for their consumers and provide other organizations access for marketing efforts. By building platforms across core functions of the internet, including search, social, and e-commerce to accomplish this dominance, these few organizations that'll be examined have regulated or destroyed the role of content in favor of data. Organizations can leverage these platforms in many ways, as this book explores. For organizations, the consumer decision journey is made more transparent and accountable with data. This allows for a more dynamic consumer decision journey over the simplicity of previous models. Here data expands the role of marketing beyond brand awareness or lead generation into experience, retention, and consumer satisfaction.

After the death of content as king, there's still a role it can play within data-driven marketing. Organizations that have embraced data have shown ways in which content can be personalized at scale directly for the consumer, instead of the masses. For organizations that look to embrace the data-revolution, it will require piecing together their data silos. The process for which to deliver meaningful impact for stakeholders necessitates establishing relationships between the organization and the consumer, data governance to ensure responsibility, and data models that theoretically can be applied to any data set in organization homes.

Even a democracy built on data isn't without risks. Privacy has become a major consumer concern related to data. High-profile data breaches have become more common and global governments respond to the changing virtual landscape by increasing regulations on organizations to protect consumers. Organizations will need to explore a more balanced approach to data and privacy that accounts for these risks by establishing trust and adapting to the various laws across the virtual data landscape.

Perhaps it was a simpler time when content was king. History, however, is written by the victors, as the adage goes. Data has won and both the consumer and organizations have benefited from this shift. Marketers, communicators, and media professionals that embrace this new data paradigm will join in the winner's circle of history, but those who don't will be forgotten.

The King that was Promised

Before a new history is written about data in this book, it's still important to look back on the era of content as king. Its reign span centuries, though, the origin of the phrase appears to begin in 1996. Bill Gates, founder of Microsoft, posted an essay on the company's website. The essay's title, *"Content is King,"* told of Gates' vision of the future for internet monetization that would mirror the previous eras of radio and television broadcasting, which he had witnessed. His observation theorized that content creators of information and entertainment would be the internet's "long-term winners." He further predicted that one day the breadth of information on the internet would be "enormous" and global in scope. He foresaw challenges ahead for content creators to be "paid for their work," for publishers the "struggle to make money" from either advertising or subscriptions, and consumer audiences should be rewarded for reading content on a screen. Although, consumer audiences would also be "less-than-thrilled about seeing advertising" that loaded slowly over dial-up internet connection speeds. He presumed opportunities for those who created content that had "depth or interactivity," like audio or video, but assumed the internet would be the "multimedia equivalent of the photocopier." It'd allow for low-cost production of content "no matter the size of the audience" at scale with ease. For Gates, the only future successful benefactors of the new internet medium would be those who created a "marketplace" from content.

The irony of the essay that coined the phrase content is king is that it's no longer available on the website where it started. Still, the Internet Archive website maintains a copy of the page as it appeared on Microsoft's website in 1996.[2] A few other websites have also examined Gates' essay as it relates to the origin of the phrase. Gates himself ignores the crown he bestowed to instead focus upon his philanthropy efforts. The company from which he retired, Microsoft, as another sign of the new era, centers its business areas around data across computer software, computer hardware, consumer electronics, social networking services, cloud computing, video games, and internet services business sectors.

The prediction that the internet would continue to follow in the footsteps of its other media counterparts was easy for Gates to assume in 1996. Content development for mass media was a pattern that had repeated for each medium since print. Both radio and television had this structure for broadcasting content. It was observational selection to assume that the internet would follow without any change in the status quo. Broadcasting and advertising already had a long history together supporting each other. So, the best way to understand the paradigm Gates observed is to briefly revisit the past.

While it's possible to go back several thousands of years before the common era (BCE) to trace the history of print on some material or another, it was perhaps the invention of the printing press by Johannes Gutenberg, around 1540 A.D., that first brought content to the masses.[3] While at first the mass production of Bibles and books took precedence in terms of content, it wasn't long before newspapers and magazines followed. The frequency and production necessitated the support of advertising to keep the presses running to produce more content. Consumer literacy became the only limiting factor in its adoption and consumption around the world.

It was almost 400 years later before another form of mass media was created, first in radio and followed within a few decades by television. Content for these new media channels wasn't static like it was for print, as continuous broadcasts required content creators to produce for as much of the standard day as possible. To hear or view this content, the consumer was only required to own radio and television sets. At first, each of these media channels was limited to local stations. But as technology allowed for nationwide broadcasting, the content being produced by media broadcasting networks improved in terms of both quality and quantity.

This was the media era of Gates' observation. The creation of content for each new medium in broadcasting was getting more expensive for both the artistic development and production, as well as the scientific-technical components of distribution. To fund these expenses, media organizations found support and funding from organizations in the form of advertisements.[4] More importantly, the relationship between content producers and marketers was by then a pattern. It had repeated itself, without fail, by 1996 and was easy to assume it'd repeat with the internet era.

In the year of Gates' essay, advertisers were spending over $175 billion in media, but no internet advertising was reported. The broadcasting of content was being well-supported with over fifty-four billion dollars of advertising expenditures across broadcast TV, cable TV, and radio categories. Print and magazine categories was over forty-seven billion dollars and was seeing growth over several previous years, while direct mail marketing represented just over thirty-four billion dollars that same year. The following year, in 1997, recorded $600 million in digital advertising. Still, less than one percent of total advertising expenditures were recorded. But there is some likelihood that it was already underway in 1996. Only, no accessible data exists for reference.[5]

The technology that would start to power digital advertising across the internet was still in its infancy during these years. The first digital advertising server to manage placement, targeting, and tracking was reportedly set up in 1995 by Focalink Communications.[6] A year before that, some of the first paid digital advertisements, a web banner, were sold by HotWired.[7] The web banner was the first advertising format that could support the content being created on the internet. And, it'd be the standard format for many years to come.

What made digital advertising instantly different from other channels was the ability to track if the advertisement had any impact. Television and radio relied on audience measurement techniques and separate research collected after the broadcast to determine ad recall. Advertisers in print and direct mail would have to use coupons or discount codes to determine if these specific channels drove any lift. Because tracking technology was built-into the formation of digital advertising, it made the medium ideal for marketers looking for a direct connection between advertising dollars and results.

Today, every sector of the modern economy has an internet presence. Moreover, marketing has followed to support it. As of 2019, the research firm eMarketer has predicted that U.S. digital ad spending would increase to $129.3 billion, while traditional advertising would fall to $109.5 billion. That means that digital accounts for 54.2% of the total, while traditional only represents 45.8%.[8] While the web banner ad is still a part of the digital advertising mix as display marketing, two decades have added technology to improve upon it. Thus, it's developed an incredible amount of other digital advertising options, including but not limited to search advertising, geofencing, retargeting, video advertising, and social media advertising.

The Sun Never Sets on the Content Empire

Gates predicted that the internet would be unimaginably large. Now, more content exists than can be consumed, and more is created every minute. Imagine the internet as Bill Gates suggested; as a marketplace. It'd be a virtual bazaar about the diameter of the largest celestial body in our solar system, the Sun. At the time of this writing, according to Internet Live Stats, part of the Real Time Statistics Project, there are over 1.9 billion websites in the world with over 4 billion internet users available to consume it.[9] Content in the form of social media posts, photos, videos, and emails are measured in terms of billions and trillions being created each year. The size of the internet is estimated to be 4.51 billion pages long, according to the website World Wide Web Size.[10] If each page was limited to a standard 8.5 by 11-inch letter page, the length would stretch over three times the distance between the Earth and the Moon. However, a webpage isn't limited to any length or width size. One webpage alone could contain all the books ever written. Therefore, no reliable measurement for how long it would take to consume all of the text, photos, videos, and other content available to the public is possible. And yet, hundreds of more websites and pages will be created before this chapter is finished — perhaps millions more before this book is published.

There's also no start to the internet marketplace. Arguably, there's no end either, because new websites are created every second. Each organization in this virtual marketplace has an address to locate their website. It consists of a combination of numbers, letters, and domain names unique to that website. Inside the organization's website storefront at this address could also be millions or billions of more web pages for every service or product the organization offers. Some of the websites in the virtual marketplace focus, not on selling, but rather keeping each consumer's attention. Then, they sell that attention to advertisers. Still, more websites provide information free to the public, provide government services or utilities for their earthbound citizens. Further yet, there are websites with intentions both legal and illegal. While some terrestrial services like banks or local restaurants may have provided their consumers with their address on the internet, the question remains: How do consumers discover new locations within this endless virtual marketplace? More importantly, how do these websites get consumer attention, hold it, and ensure the outcome that aligns with their organization's goals?

Content Marketing Regime

In the same way, location, location, location was the buzzword response from real estate agents to small businesses as the key to success. In the virtual marketplace, the mantra was content, content, content. For most of the new century, the marketing profession has unabashedly promoted content as king.

Content marketing positioned itself as the rejection of traditional advertising attention-grabbing tactics. Inbound Marketing Strategist at HubSpot, Kipp Bodnar, recalls the early era of internet marketing: "Before content, if you were a marketer, you were primarily using email and advertising to gain prospective customers. Those were the channels and, oh, did marketers use them. They so overplayed them that consumers began to adopt technology to filter them out. They blocked ads. They set up inbox filters. They reduced the noise and took control of their own purchase process."[11] The king that was promised was a free source of attention that, according to Bodnar if it was good and relevant, would find its way to provide endless customers.

Within the kingdom of content, new schools of marketing thought developed to support this era against marketing's prior forms. Consider HubSpot, a technology company with over 50,000 customers of its services across a hundred countries. They make marketing automation solutions for inbound marketing in order to create quality content, pulling an audience in where it's believed they naturally want to be while reading more content.[12] Several dozen content and inbound marketing conferences are hosted across the globe each year. There's over 3,000 books on Amazon to date, and more than 2.6 billion search results for these keyword phrases exists on Google. If history was written by victors, then the kingdom of content would appear to be vast.

No King Rules Forever

Nevertheless, the phrase content is king, like the emperor in the Hans Christian Andersen tale, hasn't any clothes. Essentially, the content hasn't any value. John Hall, entrepreneur and author, wrote on the impact of this to marketing, "Post a great article to a publication that your target buyer doesn't read and you'll achieve nothing. Although this sounds intuitive, the truth is, in many industries, sixty to seventy percent of content isn't strategically distributed. Most of it, in fact, ends up sitting idly on company blogs that few people ever visit."[13] Content is like a tree falling in the woods. If no one reads it, hears it, or sees it, then it is difficult to determine whether marketing has proved successful.

Both the rapid pace of internet expansion and the growth of the content marketing industry has signaled new dilemmas for content. Bodnar observed that as "the volume of content went up, while the quality often went down. Content farms popped up. Brands, as a result, started to fund the spread of bad content through paid channels. As content offers increased, they became less valuable, and then they crossed the line into utter noise. Good content still exists, but you have to sift through an awful lot of cheap content to get to it."[14]

As the never-ending internet increases in size and content follows, what doesn't increase is the attention span of audiences. As entrepreneur Jonathan Lacoste points out, consumers are bombarded by content, ads, offers, emails, texts, tweets, push notifications and everything else imaginable. As a whole, the industry has reached a point of "content shock" according to him, where consumers can't consume any more content than they already are.[15] Time, then, always remains a constant barrier to content marketing. And when consumers' attention spans are reportedly shorter than goldfish, less than eight seconds, marketers have even less time to attract and hold an audience.[16]

Under the economic law of supply and demand, according to Social Media Marketing Expert Mark Schaefer, the content marketing model begins to fall apart. Content creation has been exploding at a ridiculous rate as the result of content marketing creating a near-infinite supply. Meanwhile, the demand is always finite to the number of hours consumers can pay attention while still having to eat, work, drive, and live.[17] As Schaefer and others have pointed out, content marketing isn't a sustainable strategy.

The biggest problem of all is that this content doesn't have a value. How do consumers know what's worth their time and attention, when almost by design, the internet has neither anywhere to start nor finish? Jesse Kornbluth, author and internet executive, argues counter to the conventional wisdom that content is king. Thus, users overwhelmed with so many websites turned to other websites that positioned themselves as internet navigators. Consumers wanted a starting place and so certain technology companies started to fill that void.[18] The followers of content marketing would have everyone believing the problem's solution is better content, but still with no means to measure whether it was successful.

The Rise of a Data Democracy

Content as king faces an unsolvable dilemma of its own, ensuring that too much of anything loses its value. And yet, the opposite is true of another growing resource on the internet: data. Created not by marketers but by the consumers and by the websites and actions they take, internet users are monitored by technology at an increasing rate.

The amount of data available now grows faster than the internet. Ben Walker, a marketing executive at Vouchercloud, estimates that some 2.5 quintillion bytes of data are created daily on the internet.[19] Much of the data being generated has given away network effects for websites that have it. The more people that use it, the more value it gains because of the data the website has and how it uses it to improve those user experiences. The very nature of data has changed the economy according to *The Economist* magazine, "By collecting more data, a firm has more scope to improve its products. Overall, this attracts more users, generates even more data, and so on."[20] Large organizations now exist with websites and services that have become platforms built on this kind of data. Alphabet Inc. uses data to power the world's most popular search engine platform Google, the video-sharing website YouTube, Maps for navigation, the world's most widely used web browser Chrome, and many more products.[21] For Facebook and its owned mobile apps Instagram, Whatsapp, and Messenger, data influences a global community of social media platforms used by more than 2.5 billion people. Then there's Amazon, where data facilitates the largest e-commerce platform. More than half of all internet shoppers price check or began their product search, built on one of the largest cloud-computing platforms, Amazon Web Services. Not only do these platforms have an abundance of data due to internet users using them for free, but marketers have access to enough of it to target customers directly on these platforms.

Advertising agencies that have realized this trend's importance have also become big data hoarders. All are hoping to assemble data collections that attribute to improving their efforts on behalf of organizations. Marketers' advantages of being able to track online behavior, according to Former Senior GroupM Executive Brian Lesser, is that "We know what you want even before you know you want it." This sophistication is powered by the new "Math Men." It replaces the twentieth-century creative ad agency "Mad Men," which represents engineers and data scientists whose realm is machine learning, algorithms, segmented data, and artificial intelligence.[22] It identifies the results of which marketing campaigns can now be measured on actual performance metrics, specifically from consumer actions instead of relying upon estimated reach or message recall.

Platforms are both now the largest data collectors from internet users. It clarifies where the majority of marketing budgets are spent to attract those users to many organizations' products or services. Marketing decisions can be based on data at every stage of the consumer's journey. While the individual internet user can experience advertising personalized for them rather than only their demographic segments, this data occurs instantly at scale. Content is no longer a means to an end. Instead, it constitutes a variable among many that can be tested, optimized, and constructed with data. As the use of data continues to evolve at an exponential rate, it's more important than ever for organizations to understand and adapt their marketing process to this data-revolution. In the immortal words of philosopher and revolutionary Thomas Paine: "We have it in our power to begin the world over again."[23] Let us build it with data.

CHAPTER TWO

Living in the Data Democracy

Life in the age of the data democracy is often about the balance between data input and output. Like a government democracy, the quality of life in a data democracy is all about what the "citizen" or internet user puts into it. So, it's important to understand what they can get out of the available data. It's also important to understand if it's the right data, from good sources, and was understood correctly. Simply put, content alone isn't going to answer the questions important to any marketing campaign. A data democracy must be built knowing what an organization wants to achieve first. Like a real democracy, it requires structure.

If the organization was a car dealership, the goal would be to get people that are interested in buying a car on the dealership's car lot. The car inventory is going to play a large part in that process. Is every car on the lot available on the car dealership's website? Are the cars searchable by both large search engines and niche car related aggregators? Have previous car buyers from the lot been able to leave reviews via social media networks? And, are those reviews positive? Does the digital marketing lead to relevant landing pages? Do those pages allow interested car buyers to contact a salesperson and set up an appointment at the lot? Finally, is a process in place to determine which of these methods or a mix of methods results in a car purchase each day? Now, replace every mention of the car in this paragraph with another product or service, the dealership lot with either a storefront or website, or the salesperson appointment with the buying funnel. Marketers can arrive at perhaps an ideal attribution model within a data democracy. The last thing a marketer wants now is a broken or missing part of this data stream, worst yet, to be unaware that something is wrong with the data.

In many ways, my family's car buying experience last summer illustrated the possible data points of potential customers. After our mid-size SUV finally became too expensive to repair, we began the search for a new car. It was my wife's car, so it was up to her to find the car she wanted to replace it. It was my job to research the cars she found and deal with the salesperson when we got to the lot.

Her car buying experience started on social media, inquiring on Facebook with friends. One family she chatted with on Messenger had owned nothing but Nissan cars with only positive comments, while another family from a Facebook group spoke highly of that brand, specifically the Nissan Altima. We had only owned Toyota cars, as a family, so I started researching the brand and car model, while my wife started looking for used cars nearby. At this point, we were both searching on Google. Within a few days, she had located a few options that fit our needs and she sent emails through the dealer's website to set-up test drives.

On my way home from work that evening, my wife called me to say, she was satisfied with the test drive. So, I should come to the lot and to work with the salesman. Within an hour of negotiations, we had a deal. While we waited for the paperwork to be processed, the salesman handed my wife a survey that his manager required for all transactions. I instantly recognized the questions: a simple "How did you hear about us?" marketing survey with a few additional media habit questions. At this point in the evening, my wife was exhausted and just shrugged it off, not wanting to deal with it. I wasn't interested either as I was still busy reviewing the buyer's loan agreements. Then something happened that shocked me. The salesman grabbed the survey back from my wife and proceeded to fill it out on his own. His work was a complete fabrication regarding how we heard about them, our media habits, and any other additional questions I couldn't see from my point of view. My shock turned to disgust, realizing that this was bad data for marketers trying to support this car dealership. They wouldn't have any idea the data they had was false. Worse yet, how many times that day, week, month, or even year had the salesman falsified the data in the survey? *Were other salespeople at the lot were doing the same?* I wondered.

In order for a data to function as a democracy for marketing, the source of that data must be understood. It must be as true of a representative of the will of the consumer as possible. It's meaning devoid of emotional bias, leaving as much as can be achievable, through pure logic.

If a Tree Falls in the Woods, Was Marketing Responsible?

Let's first dispose of the fallacy that the salesman in my wife's car buying experience was the only point of failure in the marketing survey. It was also the question, "How did you hear about us?" It's the most basic of questions, which for marketers, should tell if the marketing campaigns are working. Does it drive the awareness and the customer into the sales funnel? However, every modern marketer should know that it isn't that simple because the problem is looking for a single point of attribution for marketing success. The question, even if my wife answered it herself, would have relied on her memory of what led her to the car lot that evening, instead of the actual data of the journey. The attribution for our particular car buying experience was across several platforms, which for marketers, leaves a more complex network of data elements to consider.

For marketing, attribution plays a critical role in determining which strategies are successful. Several models exist for attribution, ranging from simplistic single source attribution to sophisticated multi-source attribution (fig. 2.1). Single source models, the credit for marketing success, is usually assigned to either the First Click Model or the initial interaction where the lead engaged. Alternatively, it could be assigned to the Last Click Model interaction where the lead completed the action. Neither of these models give any credit to other interactions that occur and too much credit to the one that does, which is their main flaw. Still, they are the easiest to track. Multi-source attribution models attempt to take into account every interaction with the lead, weighted against different parts of the consumer's funnel. The variations are based on what part of attribution the marketer may want to track. The First and Last Click Model splits the majority of interaction weight against those interactions while also giving minor credit to interactions that occur between them. A Linear Model gives equal weight to all interactions. The Time Decay Model gives more credit to the most recent inaction and less to all the previous in reverse order. A Custom Model assigns weight based on the marketers or organizations preferences or priorities.[1] The difficult part is figuring out which model is ideal, since none of the technology currently available can track the entire consumer funnel both online and offline.

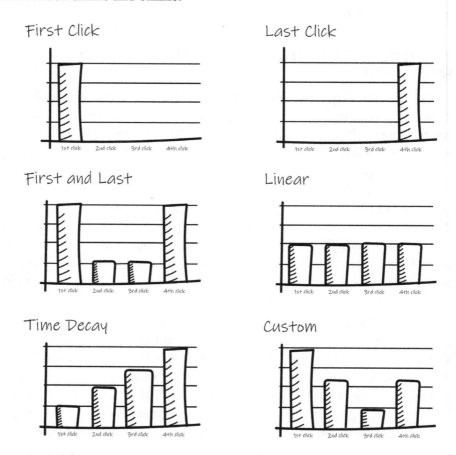

Figure 2.1. Illustrations by team Charcoal of models from Rheinlander, Scott. "Everything You Wanted to Know About Marketing Attribution Models (but Were Afraid to Ask)." Salesforce Blog, April 19, 2019. https://www.salesforce.com/blog/2017/11/what-is-marketing-attribution-model.html.

With all the data that's available, it's important to find the signal within the noise within any given attribution model. Channels that appear the most often across different models are valuable and should be nurtured. A mix of paid and earned sources will give an indication of the health of both brand awareness and the effectiveness of paid messages. Meanwhile, a moderate amount of skepticism and repeat testing will ensure the model doesn't become outdated by any change in the habits of consumers.

Within a data democracy, attribution should be considered part of the framework upon which the entire foundation is justified. The key intersection occurs between data, marketing, and results. The right attribution model will validate all parts of a data-driven marketing campaign, from which the audience interacts with platforms. The organization's platforms indicate to what levels of the consumer's funnel each of them is at, and then what variables of personalization make the most impact. Incorrect models will lead to marketing results that do not scale. Channels that show false positives will garner more resources but then show no increases in return on investment.

The data inside attribution models favor facts and not memory. Asking a consumer to remember every interaction with a brand before purchasing will result in incomplete data sets. Although, asking them to select only one answer to "How did you hear about us?" will likely result in an answer they most desire to give; as consumers will rarely want to admit an advertisement is what influenced their decision.

The 5 W's

Content does little within an attribution model other than providing another data point. Again, the value for marketers in creating content as the main focus of activities was always dubious at best. Only the data can determine the who, what, where, when, and why for content. The content on the web page as text, audio, or video can't answer any simple questions. Its only purpose and function is to be consumed. Only the data can provide value from it.

Who? Content about to be consumed has no clue who the audience is that views or listens to it. It might be an article written for tourists visiting Seattle for the first time that's mainly used by teachers in Seattle looking for field-trip ideas. Any and all attributes of who the audience is can only be simulated by whom the content was made primarily for. Conversely, data analytics can provide the likely location, age, gender, annual household income, family status, and more from the internet user.

What? Content can't tell what was consumed by the audience. The entire article, the top half of the screen, the first few seconds of the video, or other sections of content on the same website. Data can determine the length of time on a website, how far the internet user got on the page, or how many pages they visited on a website. If there was media on the webpage, data could tell how much of it was played, when it was paused, and if the song or video was given a positive or negative rating.

Where? Content is unable to determine where the audience was before it arrived or where it went after it finished. Was this the first website the audience visited when visiting the web? Did another piece of content refer them, or was it another platform? After they are finished with the content, did they stay on the website to see more content, make a purchase, or leave? Again, the data is able to provide the prior source of the audience's visit to the website, determine what marketing or non-marketing channels sent them and if they exited to the desired goal.

When? Content doesn't know what time it is because the internet never closes. As long as the web server that is hosting the content is up and running, it is always available to any audience around the globe. Yet, content can't determine when the audience arrived, left, or even how often they view it. With data, each visit is recorded. It determines when or if the user returns, and how long it has been since that visit.

Why? Content can't answer the most important question: Why did the audience care about it? Was it the result of marketing efforts? Was it something for which they were searching and found? Did a friend recommend it? The list of why they found it is endless. And yet, the data can seek to answer the why by creating those plausible correlations between digital marketing and other points of available data as just about every interaction on the internet can be measured and attributed.

Form Follows Function

A data democracy is defined in many of the same ways an actual democracy functions within a government. However, democracy has not always been defined the same way. In fact, it can mean different things to different people at different periods in time.[2] In order to fit data within this form of government, it's important to reach a consensus on what attributes a data democracy follows. The Center for Civic Education states the shared attributes of a democracy today are popular sovereignty, majority rule with minority rights, individual rights, free and open elections, citizen involvement and open compromise.[3]

The first attribute, popular sovereignty and the right to govern, is given by the people in a democracy. In a data democracy, the power of the data comes directly from internet users. It acts as their vote, determining what websites are most important to each user. Internet users can then generally continue to use that website for as long as it provides them some value, abandon it for another, or perhaps remove themselves from it. Thus, it denies that website any ongoing value from data.

In a democracy, the second attribute, majority rule, is created where the most votes are given. In the data democracy, the platforms with the most data rule the internet. Unlike a government democracy, this is not a one-party rule. Major platforms exist on the internet across different sectors like search, social, and e-commerce. Within each sector, minority rights for smaller platforms do exist like Microsoft's Bing to Alphabet's Google for search, Twitter to Facebook for social, and just about every other website operating an e-commerce store against Amazon.

Perhaps the least developed part of the data democracy to date is the third attribute, individual rights and its connection to privacy. Data flows freely on the internet from its users to many different websites, platforms, and systems; however, very few regulations govern this exchange depending on what economic sector or country the data originated in or is currently stored. Less so data is outside the user's direct control. Chapter nine will explore ways to consider and establish privacy guidelines for data.

For the fourth attribute, free and open elections, it's important to consider that every second internet users are participating in elections, they will use their data. What websites to visit, what platforms to use, products to buy, and where to shop are all election-based decisions. These ongoing data-election choices are free and open because nothing is forcing the user towards their destination, or requiring that once they start using a website, they must do anything that is required by it. With data, each of these elections, are now visible to the marketer. It allows them to understand better the choices or non-choices that were made, enabling different marketing tactics to then be used based on either the last completed or the next future election requiring their data vote.

People making data available by their own virtue of being internet users satisfies one of the final attributes, citizen involvement. While open compromise is the reality that websites should be personalized to each user, since it requires some form of data exchange. The level of citizen participation is up to them.

There are differences between a data democracy for internet users and democracy as a form of government for people. For starters, there is no official constitutional document for the data democracy, which acts as the initial starting point for many government democracies. Websites have their terms of service, but these are designed by lawyers to protect the company, not the internet users. Perhaps unwittingly from the user's point of view, they have signed a new social contract in the digital age. Platforms, advertisers, and users exchange value as a mix of data, dollars. An engagement has become more valuable as platforms grow and network effects have kicked in.[4] Other universal principles for a democracy, like checks and balances or the rule of law, exist only in the abstract when it comes to data without an original binding common law.

The function of the data democracy is best positioned in the way it works because of the representation. The opposite was true in 1999 when ICANN, Internet Corporation for Assigned Names and Numbers, attempted to bring actual democracy to the internet. Users from around the world elected delegates to represent their continent as at-large members of the ICANN Board of Directors. The structure of the internet, they proposed, would then be governed by its users. The experiment failed as only a fraction of internet users at the time participated in the elections.[5] Why a data democracy works today is because people feel they are being understood. Websites are better at understanding user needs and aligning those needs with the website's goals. Because this understanding is powered by algorithms and web servers operating at fractions of a second, it appears effortless and completely user responsive. A sharp contrast to prior mediums, where the media-industry was focused on only creating and broadcasting content for consumption. This generation of data-driven platforms is all about studying user behavior to make improvements for their users.

The Struggle of the Old Guard

Ted Leonsis, former president of AOL, now founder and partner at Revolution Growth, wrote that the rapid pace of change with the internet hasn't left any part of the media industry untouched. Instead, it was forced to deal with technology disruption. That technology has changed how content was created, what it cost, who produced it, and where you could watch it. But more importantly, it has changed how it was discovered and shared.[6] All the while, the internet was viewed in the beginning by the media industry as just another medium of awareness that could be supported by traditional advertising models. They likely soon realized it was a loss. Leaders as consumers, at first, weren't willing to pay a subscription for anything. Digital advertising revenue was minuscule compared to other formats. The problem was the explosion of internet users. Less than one percent of the world's population was online around the time of Gates' essay. Now, the population is estimated around forty percent or four billion people.[7] For news, publishers, and entertainment, that is a lot of eyeballs worthy of attention.

The news was a natural fit for the early internet, since both were limited to written text content before browsing technology improved. The struggle was that local and network news outlets were previously the gatekeepers of what deserved attention on any given day. Search and social media platforms changed, which made all content from anywhere accessible and shareable across the globe. What followed from 2000 to 2015 was coined the "Print Apocalypse" by American journalist Derek Kahn Thompson. Forty billion dollars in newspaper advertising revenue fell, wiping out the gains of the previous fifty years.[8] The giants and conglomerate of old that have survived, do so at the mercy of search and social platforms that send the majority of internet traffic to their websites. Their struggle today is attempting to limit the consumption of news content to push readers towards subscription models, while still hoping to get as much attention as possible with each breaking news cycle.

Publishers faced their own technological distribution nightmare in the form of another platform, Amazon. Before, publishers not only decided who got published, they also set the list price for the books, and selling to bookstores at a discount. The stores would sell them at list price to make a profit. Amazon had long exploited price as a weapon in the marketplace, discounting heavily to favor customer acquisition and retention over immediate margin and profits.[9] Amazon followed this dominance up with a widely successful eBook device enabling them to access content from small niche publishers. It further extended the growing trend of self-publishers, who could avoid the costly print and distribution channels for a larger return on investment with eBooks.

The entertainment industry within media fought against the distribution of the internet with other tactics, such as lawsuits and licensing. Initial music social networks like Napster, where users could share their music collection with others freely, came under a barrage of copyright lawsuits that tried to delay the entertainment industry from losing a grip on their content. Eventually, they licensed their music catalogs to be made available on Apple's iTunes store under protected formats. The distribution of video was at first hamstrung by the early internet's dial-up speeds, but as digital media formats like Flash made it easier to view a video in a web browser, and broadband internet speeds increased, platform's like YouTube soon dominated video consumption. For video, the media industry tried several solutions. It licensed content to be purchased or subscribed to via services and websites like iTunes and Netflix. Eventually, they went to ad-supported practices with content partnerships like Hulu and media networks enabling their own websites to broadcast content.

The focus on how the content was consumed left the media industry unprepared for how data would dominate the distribution across the internet. Technology writer John Herrman argues that all these worries stem from a transfer of power: from publisher to platform; from content creator to content distributor. In exchange for an audience, platforms asked for some degree of labor, conformity, and control.[10] This power manifests itself in both the amount of traffic the major platforms receive to disburse and the amount of advertising and e-commerce revenue these platforms absorb in comparison to the media industry.

No Such Thing as a Free Lunch

In his observations on the media industry during the golden age of television, artist Richard Serra said that, "If you aren't paying for a product, you are the product."[11] This observation was true during the broadcast era, and has scaled to global extremes during the data democracy era. For internet users, this means free access to search engines that crawl the entire internet, social media networks that span over most of the world, and access to e-commerce storefronts with near endless variety. It also means they are the product if they use these platforms and websites whether they want to be or not.

In return, internet users can receive a more personalized web experience. Search results can be built on not only prior keyword searches but the actions taken on the search result pages and the websites they visit. Social networks can connect people to long lost friends and family far away, while also helping find people to fall in love with. Untethering the physical limitations of offerings in retail spaces and eliminating waiting times in cashier lines, causes less than knowledgeable support staff to replace it with an always available e-commerce stores offering everything imaginable with fast shipping option.

Beyond free platforms, even paid platforms have transformed data points into disruption and personalization. Netflix has over 100 million paid subscribers on their media-streaming platform. Every search their subscribers make, every positive or negative rating they give, and every show or movie watched is correlated with third-party sources like Nielsen rating data. Every device logged onto the platform from any location is associated with licensing data, directors, actors, plots, themes and more.[12] In turn, Netflix is able to turn subscriber movie habits into both content development by region and targeted marketing to retain current subscribers and attract new ones, which is why Netflix now has more subscribers than cable television.[13]

Only those that have mastered the principles of a data democracy have benefited from this dynamic of internet users as products. It isn't simply having them become registered users or paying customers. It's about collecting data to improve that experience for each user that follows, reporting at scale. Nor is it just having the data on spreadsheets or charts but actionable intelligence with models that are tested and retested. While the power in a data democracy stems from the user, it also flows to those that can then use the data for marketing and their organizations.

The Value to Marketing

The three factors that present the most value to marketing in a data democracy are targeting, price, and accountability. While these factors don't represent the only value that marketing can find in data, their combination is the minimum requirement. Restrictions that existed in the prior media channels no longer apply to this new era as the result of tracking. After all, the limitations that were once placed on marketing teams for accountability no longer apply.

A forever adage of perfect marketing strategy was finding the right audience with the right message at the right time, the first part of which is targeting an audience. However, in publishing or broadcasting, there is no guarantee that the desired audience is paying attention. It's only the *possibility* of a future audience paying attention. The advantage of targeting on platforms is that marketers can be sure the audience is searching or browsing exactly at the moment an ad appears. This leaves marketing teams to determine what is the right target audience to deliver the appropriate message that correlates with the target's location in the consumer's funnel.

Before platforms dominated, advertising prices were largely set by the publishers or the stations at a fixed rate. Now, however, platforms use auction house style bidding for advertisers to win ad placement, leaving price as a fluctuating barometer of factors. The prior channels were limited by the number of pages in a publication or ads available during airtime, allowing premium prices to be set with limited supply. Platforms in search have nearly unlimited keyword combinations. Those in social have massive network effects of billions of people, allowing supply to be near limitless while forcing small and big firms to always be competing for price in their advertising auctions. This forces marketing teams to constantly pay attention to price, making sure the right target audience is being delivered the right message within the marketing budget.

Finally, with accountability, the structure of the data democracy comes full circle in its value. The attribution models created from tracking the right data sources provide marketers with the answers to the questions they have asked for at least a century, but does the marketing work? Prior channels could not provide those answers within the boundaries of the media, requiring separate market research. Now marketing teams with access to the right data attribution models can understand the optimal price to target the optimal audience and determine the right platforms to advertise on.

CHAPTER THREE

A Platform by Any Other Name

The next three chapters focus on what makes certain platforms critical to a successful data democracy. It's important to explain what a platform is within the context of this book, what makes them different than websites, and how a platform must be accessible for marketing for it to be part of a data democracy. In the early years of the internet, interactions between users and websites were primarily one directional. An internet user visited a website using a web browser from a computer. The web browser made a request for the website stored on the associated web server, and the server would ideally respond, sending back the code for the web browser to display to the user. The web pages were mostly static; though as time passed, each of these layers improved and allowed for dynamic interactions with websites. The key was the ability for data to not only be bi-directional but also omnidirectional, sending and receiving multiple data sets by means of data algorithms. These could vary based on the internet user's interaction. Platforms, then, are a series of web services across one or more websites that are an interaction between users, data algorithms, and web server databases that generate data sets unique to the individual user.

Platforms are different from other websites on the internet, not just by the collection of data and use of algorithms but rather the focus on improving the experience for the user. If the platform fails the user, it can fail forward by improving the experience for the very next user using algorithms. If a website's content fails a user, the website's owner has to create new content for the next users. Generally, this is completed without knowing how they failed the previous user with content.

The advantage of dominant platforms is how they make data accessible to organizations for marketing. Whether it is the keywords of Google, the audiences of Facebook, or product promotion on Amazon, by allowing organizations to target users of these platforms, it helps the user discover something they might need. The organization discovers a new consumer. The platform benefits by both the repeated use of users and the influx of marketing dollars from other organizations. Platforms can then leverage these additional resources to both improve the experiences of users and provide more access to organizations. Author, startup advisor, and angel investor Matt Ward wrote that Google, Facebook, and Amazon are today's most valuable companies. Ultimately, it is no coincidence they are all platforms. Platforms have the advantage of pricing power and aggregate the majority of value.[1]

Because users are the platforms' product, it makes sense that platforms should be investing in improving that product. And yet, it also makes sense that, within a data democracy, it's important for those platforms that users have voted to reward them with improvements. Either way, the main goal of any platform in a data democracy is to keep the user happy. The three most dominant platforms in search (Google), social (Facebook), and e-commerce (Amazon) achieved this status by removing the value from content in order to find it in data.

Pick a Color – Any Color

I've always felt like my career could be summed up by the motto, "If something wasn't broke, I wouldn't be here to fix it." After leaving the casino industry for higher education, it felt especially relevant considering the state of the university that hired me. In an era of dwindling state appropriations, shrinking high school populations in the state causing decreasing enrollment, and growing competition both locally and nationally, the University of Missouri-St. Louis (UMSL) had also neglected to redesign their website in almost a decade. At the speed the internet was moving in 2010, it might as well have been a century.

Of course, like any new job, I was on UMSL's employee probationary period for my first six months, during which time they could fire me without cause. I still remember that, after more than five years working there, my mission on day one was to launch the first new web redesign before my six months were up. Otherwise, I could forget about month seven. To UMSL's credit, I wasn't starting from scratch. The university had understood the need for a new website two years prior. They had already started an executive web committee to begin the process, and by the time I arrived, they had a new design almost ready to go.

And yet, nothing about getting this new web design launch was going to be easy if my first meeting with the executive web committee was any indication. Creatives from the marketing department had managed to spend the bulk of an hour-long meeting arguing with the web developers from the IT department about what color the border around a textbox on the homepage should be. The IT department wanted to lock in the design; therefore, they could start coding it into the new content management system. The creatives in marketing wanted to mockup three to five color options to review. I knew then, we were going to be in trouble if this continued.

Nothing about the color of the border was going to impact how many students the university was going to have next year. Nor did the color impact any of the decisions a student was going to have to make before deciding if UMSL was for her or him. The color around the textbox wasn't going to impact navigation on the website or where they went to apply to the university. The color wasn't going to impact how people felt about the university and no student was going to tell their friends about that color. The color had no impact on how students would find the university's website. The color simply didn't matter, because nobody outside that room was going to care. And, nothing significant would come of it.

After the meeting, I asked permission from UMSL's Chief Marketing Officer if I could decide when the committee meets again and run any major decisions for his approval only. He quickly agreed to both requests. After that, the executive web committee group never met again for the entire five years of my tenure. The university's new website design launched less than five months later.

In the end, the only choices that mattered were those that enabled UMSL to enroll more students. That meant more applications from more qualified students. More students had to come from somewhere. To me, it was more logical to find more students from existing sources, where they were already finding UMSL, then try to figure out completely new sources of students. UMSL's website already had more students finding it from search engine results than other sources of traffic. And so, the first step in building a data-driven approach to marketing started with search engine platforms.

Let Me Google That for You

Google's search engine wasn't the first search engine on the internet, nor after it was launched in 1998 would it be the last or only search engine to exist. While the history of search engines on the internet is comparable to world history being filled with conflict and superpowers vying for domination within the industry, the aftermath over twenty years later is that, as a search platform, Google has no equal. At the start of 2019, Google search dominated other search engines by over ninety percent in user market share. It was the number one website in the world in terms of traffic, and process billions and billions of search queries each day.[2] And if that wasn't enough, Google owns a plethora of vertical search services in news, maps, video, and more that not only act as standalone search engines for each area but also mix into Google search results. Plus, there's an array of popular websites, services, and software. These include the number one video sharing platform YouTube, the largest free email provider platform Gmail, the biggest web browser by market share Chrome, and the most installed smartphone mobile operating system, Android.

How Google's platforms maintain their dominance isn't just about the amount of web traffic they get or searches that are done. Rather, it's about how they use the data for their users. For starters, Google search engine is always crawling the searchable internet, going to each website, visiting each web page linked from that website, and then scanning the content on them. The results are then stored in Google's database, categorized by keywords from the content it crawled. Each webpage is then ranked for relevance by Google's proprietary data algorithms.[3]

While not all of the factors that are part of Google's data algorithms are available, several factors are known. These include what language is used, the country where the search is performed, the location of the search query, and the type of device used for the search. Then, from the user, their previous search and click data, recent searches, and past behavior are all taken into consideration. From the websites that are relevant to their site link authority, site reputation, on-page relevancy to the keywords, then from the search itself the parallel intent of that search compared to similar searches, helps to integrate results from other ranking factors.[4] These interactions occur within fractions of a second to return a unique data set of search results customized to that user's search query.

As the complexity and secrecy behind how Google's search platforms have grown, the relative reasons why a user may search might be easier to classify. The taxonomy of a search query could be broken down into three categories, according to Andrei Broder, currently a distinguished scientist at Google, formerly a research fellow and vice president of computational advertising for Yahoo!. Before that, he was the vice president of research for AltaVista. He noted that searches could include information about a topic, perform transactional searches to reach a site where further interaction could happen like shopping, or navigational searches which went to a specific destination online or offline.[5] At the time of his original research in 2002, Broder stated that there was not an assumption of intent for each query. However, the advances in search since then, as it relates to user profiles on platforms as large as Google, have likely bridged the gap to discern intent at the user level. This places Google's dominance as a search platform above all challenges. TechCrunch writer Devin Coldewey states, "As the leader and standard in search, advertising, and a number of other fundamental areas, Google is able to wield itself like a weapon."[6]

Et Tu, Google

If there was a church within the kingdom of content, then Google search was the faith with which its citizens prayed to be blessed. For marketers to be the receivers of the popular platforms, search traffic was always a goal of content marketing campaigns. The strategy of search engine optimization (SEO) was to get specific web pages to rank high on search engine result pages (SERP) for relevant keywords. The web pages would then see near endless organic (free) search traffic for as long as those keywords were relevant to the audience looking for it.

Once marketers understood the organic traffic possibilities of billions of search queries potentially leading users to their websites, they wanted every possible advantage to rank high on the SERP. At first, the platform provided the key to mastering SEO on Google search within another free tool called Google Analytics. Google Analytics allows marketers to track and report on all website traffic from any source, including search. Originally, Google Analytics also provided the individual keyword data for which searches lead users to the website, quickly becoming the favorite tool in the SEO toolbox. HubSpot Chief Marketing Officer Kipp Bodnar argued that it was what made content marketing so exciting. If a website didn't have enough authority to win a top spot in the SERP for highly competitive keywords, there were any number of keyword variations they could shoot for. Still, in his opinion, this led to high volumes of mediocre content.[7]

But the platform giveth, and the platform taketh away. In 2011, Google started hiding search keyword data in Google Analytics for signed in users of their platform. By 2013, that criteria expanded to include all Google search keyword data.[8] Google positioned the move as privacy protection for its users, however, Google didn't hide keyword data related to their Google AdWords (now Google Ads). Instead, keyword advertising focused on the product within the platform. Skepticism shortly followed that Google was making a move against the entire SEO industry, which was making billions of dollars at that point — none of which went to Google.

Whatever the motive, this platform update effectively put the SEO industry behind the curve, lacking data from the search source to provide clients. As business blogger Ann Smarty wrote, this did signal that Google wanted to put a damper on SEO. They had determined it was skewing the results in a way unhelpful to its users. "Google didn't want the SEO industry playing games with its search result rankings, and what Google wants — especially in a case like this — Google gets."[9] What remained after the update was that Google still had access to the data, providing only a single controlled access point for marketers inside their online advertising platform Google Ads.

Everything is Connected

In much the same way that Google search is more than just a search engine today; Google Ads is more than just an online advertising service for the search engine. Google Ads is itself a platform within a platform, where the users are marketers. Meanwhile, the algorithms and databases are the connected services from across Google's numerous and popular sites. These include Google Search, YouTube, Gmail and more. Because a platform always has to be improving, so has Google Ads. Expanded from the initial offering of keyword-based search ads for Google Search include digital marketing options across the majority of Google-owned properties, but also much of the known internet and the devices connected to it. This allows Google Ads to position itself as a way to connect the previous siloed aspect of the internet into one platform for marketers.

Google Ads currently offers five online advertising campaign options across the platform.

The first option is The Search Network which is the sole channel for Google search ads. But, it also includes Google Maps, Shopping, and other search sites that partner with Google. Search partners are websites that use Google's search technology to power search on their website while allowing Google Ads on those search result pages. There is no complete list of search partners that allow Google Ads, according to keyword researcher Joseph Shih. Yet, it does include large popular sites like YouTube and the New York Times along with any site using Google Custom Search. As of 2019, there are over 178,000 live websites using Google Custom Search, which means a lot of potential search partners for marketers.[10]

The next option on Google Ads is The Display Network that includes YouTube, Blogger, and Gmail. It further reaches beyond Google properties to include over two million websites and reach an estimated ninety percent of Internet users.[11] For the websites using the Google Display Network, it can be a way to make additional revenue with web traffic, without the overhead of creating their own online ad servers and ad sales operations. For large publishers who already sell advertising space on their websites, Google Display Network offers an opportunity to sell leftover inventory, or remnant space, at lower prices than the publishers' sales team.[12] For marketers, this means Google Ads can follow. It can find internet users not just on Google search but most of the internet as well.

The third option on Google Ads is The Google Shopping Network, which is a combination of the Google Merchant Center that allows other websites to enable their product feeds as searchable within Google. It's an advertising option that allows those same products to be promoted with advertising and tracked for conversion. Amazon will be the major e-commerce platform featured in chapter five. It's intended for websites that do not want to sell their products on Amazon and would rather self-host their products through the Google Merchant Center, thereby providing a valuable alternative linked to the largest search platform. Google Ads then enables marketers to build shopping campaigns that are different from

Google Search ads in that they are not based on keywords but rather bids created from the product feeds of the website.[13]

For marketers looking for an alternative to traditional broadcast television, the next Google Ads option, video campaigns, is a great fit. It includes the most popular video website on the internet, YouTube. Consider that, as of 2019, internet video traffic accounted for eighty percent of all consumer internet traffic. YouTube already reaches over a billion users, almost one-third of total Internet users; therefore, it is a well-positioned video platform.[14] More so if the marketer's target audience is teens, since teens on average spend thirty-four percent of their video time watching YouTube, more than any other online video site. Moreover, teens spend twice the amount of time-consuming YouTube than live TV.[15] The Google Ad formats for YouTube offers several options including skippable in-stream ads, where the video ads play. After five seconds, the viewer has an option to skip the ad. There's also non-skippable in-stream ads where viewers don't have the option to skip but are limited to fifteen seconds or less, as well as discovery ads that consist of a thumbnail image from the video with some text inviting internet users to click to watch the video. Bumper ads are unskippable six seconds or shorter and plays before, during, or after another video; while outstream mobile-only ads begin playing with the sound off. Viewers must interact with the ad to unmute.[16] The ad formats vary cost to the marketer based on what amount of the video was viewed or if actions were taken.

For marketers with a smartphone application as their product or service, the final option on Google Ads is the universal app campaign type. For Google, the benefit of having the most installed smartphone mobile operating system, Android, is having a large smartphone application store user base on Google Play to go along with it. Google Ads enables a campaign to be built to drive application installs across all of Google's properties. More importantly, this style of campaign works on both mobile and desktop, enabling marketing to be present on every size screen and device. Mobile users can install the application directly from the ad unit, while desktop users can remotely install the application on their mobile device for the next time they use it.

All these Google Ads options are far from limited regarding that multiple combinations can be used to determine what best benefits the organization, product or service. Beyond Google Ads, the campaign options listed above the platform offers extensions functionality, deep analytics, and flexibility that makes a specialization in Google Ads a well-respected field within digital marketing. Perhaps the most useful feature for any marketer looking to harness their data within this platform is the use of retargeting and customer matching. With retargeting, campaigns can target users that have previously visited the organization's website and create dynamic ads tailored to what the user browsed on the web. This means that marketing campaigns don't have to stop at driving the user to the website but can keep advertising to them for the entire consumer's journey. With customer match, the data that internet users have already shared with marketers can be used to target ads to reach and engage with them across the platform. In this way, marketers don't have to hope that the media channel they are using will reach their customers again like they do with print, radio or television, but rather actually find them, and only them. While not a unique feature to Google Ads, both retargeting and customer matching technology is a critical part of how the data democracy enables marketers to follow users across platforms and through the consumer's journey. This will be expanded upon in chapter six.

A common thread amongst all campaign options, channels, and tactics of Google Ads is the interwoven nature of Google Search into everything. Of course, this has always been the central focus of Google from the start and the major strength of this platform over other search engines. When looking to leverage this platform, consideration should be given to understanding these connections. Additionally, what approaches to take in order to be successful should be considered. By knowing what to solve for in search, the different ways keywords can be structured. Understanding the importance of brand versus non-brand strategies, and the enhanced importance of location targeting, marketers in a data democracy can more than survive on this platform. They can thrive.

Solve for Intent

For a marketer, the first approach to advertising on Google search is to assume what Broder wouldn't: intent. Understand that it's all about choice. Internet users have to make a choice when searching on Google search, in regard to which keywords to use. Google search, by design, requires active participation by the user as it relates to what is being searched. So, advertising can be focused on that activity. By using Broder's research on search categories of information, interaction, and navigation, any organization that would benefit from these areas can solve for intent using Google Ads.

The internet is often described as the information superhighway. The Google search platform becomes the first stop on that journey. Organizations should consider what information people would want when considering a purchase of their product or service. Then, use target keywords and keyword phrases that are connected to that information. One approach would be to develop keyword phrases based on the "5 Ws" of who, what, where, when, and why around the searches that are possible. Another approach could be to find which secondary websites contain research or reviews of the product or service and target combination keyword phrases of that website's name and the product or service category. Make no assumptions about what information is trivial or unnecessary. Instead, let the data from the keyword search campaigns determine what is most effective in reaching the audience.

While a transactional approach may be as simple as using the product or service, related keywords or the brand name of the website, a more complex approach is considering what transactions are related or necessary for the consumer. Products or services that require insurance are a good example of a related and sometimes necessary transaction that can be targeted. Accessories categories is another, where for example, if a user has just purchased a phone, they may start searching for a phone case, headphones, or chargers. If not sure what transaction relations exist for the product or service begin by looking at website analytics data, specifically what sites are referring traffic that ends in a purchase then work backward to determine the connections.

With regards to the navigational approach, it's important to consider the destination location. If the product or service purchase point is strictly offline, then the section later in this chapter on the importance of location data will be directly relevant. Online navigation, however, is looking if the intent is to go to another website of a competitor. Thus, it creates a keyword approach to incept that traffic, or if the intent is to find a relevant webpage within a large website. Marketers with an abundant array of products or services can set up a variety of keyword groups that directly lead to a specific webpage or the categories where they might be found.

When looking to solve for intent on Google search or within the multiple services that exist across the platform, Google provides tools like Keyword Planner and Google Analytics to assist with this effort. With Keyword Planner inside Google Ads, marketers can research the specific product or services to find the relevant keyword suggestions as well as the monthly search volume, estimated keyword bid, and level of competition. Brad

Smith, with AdEspresso, writes that Keyword Planner excels at helping to understand intent because users are always actively searching for solutions.[17] Marketers can build different keyword groups based on the various intent solutions for their product or service. Using Google Analytics tracks the activity from the Google Ads campaign on the organizations website. The keyword groups that path towards actionable goals are likely the closest to the intent of the consumer. Neither tools alone can provide this data insight but together provide a holistic intent path from search to action. Data again has the largest role to play for marketers in determining intent for a campaign at the start of planning, during the campaign to measure response, and at the end for tracking analytic success.

Knowing which keywords are associated with an organization's products or services doesn't necessarily equal understanding of consumer intent. After all, there might be hundreds or even thousands of keywords to consider in a campaign. Marketers may even find that various products or services are already heavily competing with other organizations for the same keywords. This can drive up the keyword bidding in Google Ads, leaving marketers no close to discerning intent. Still, other keywords may drive more clicks, at cost, but no conversions. Thankfully, marketers don't have to test every single keyword in a campaign to find the answers. Google Ads allows for various keyword match types to be used like broad, phrase, exact, and negative to add as criteria within a campaign.

Broad match keywords include close variations to the keyword selected, the widest possible inclusion. The keywords don't have to be present but associated within the search criteria (e.g., women's evening shoes broad match might include buy ladies dress shoes or fancy women's shoes). Broad match keywords can also include modifiers that look for additional words before, after, or between terms (e.g., +women +shoes modifiers might include women's shoes and socks or fashion shoes for ladies). Phrase match keywords include matches plus close variants with the same meaning (e.g., "women's evening shoes" phrase might include black women's evening shoes or lady's evening shoes on sale). The exact match looks for keywords with the same meaning and is the most targeted a match option can be (e.g., [women's evening shoes] exact keywords might include women's evening shoes, ladies evening shoes or evening shoes for women). While the negative match will exclude ads from appearing when those keywords are searched (e.g., -women's socks would not include those keywords in the shoe campaign).[18] Unlike content that cannot tell which keywords sent consumers to a website, data within Google Ads can tell. The keyword data can be tracked from the SERP to the website and follow the consumer all the way to the conversion goal. From this data, marketers can continuously improve their understanding of intent.

Brand vs. Non-Brand

An almost universal function of marketing is to drive brand awareness since there are few products or services that exist without competition. While there are many factors that lead to brand awareness, it is well recognized that awareness is the first stage of the consumer's journey towards a purchase according to advertising scholars.[19] For search engines, a brand name is still just words that act as keywords. Without keyword data from Google Analytics for organic traffic, marketers are left with few clues as to whether brand awareness was a factor in their search traffic. Because brand names are keywords, they can also be used as part of paid search campaigns along with non-brand keywords for the product or service, the data from which can help determine what factors brand awareness played in a consumer's journey, if any.

My own experience with running paid search campaigns using brand-keywords and non-brand keywords, led to an article I co-wrote with UMSL's chief marketing officer for *Currents*, a Council for Advancement and Support of Education magazine. At the time, UMSL used paid search as one of many marketing channels in a strategy that supported traditional media advertising. The paid search campaigns were composed of both brand-keywords and non-brand keywords. In one campaign, we used brand-keywords for the UMSL Day open house, tracking hits to a microsite and monitoring conversions as event registrations. The initial results were impressive. Some seventy-five percent of registrations were coming from brand-keywords. UMSL Day reached its attendance capacity several days before the event, but the percentage of attendees rose only two percent from the previous event. We noted these results and moved to the next campaign for UMSL's summer school. Again, the brand-keywords were tracking to increases in enrollment over ten percent, and yet again, the enrollment only increased less than half of what was projected. On the surface, the campaigns were successful, but the data analytics was confusing. Both campaigns showed high conversions directly from branded search keywords. And yet, the overall increases didn't correlate with increases in the paid search campaigns budget. As we continued to experiment with ad frequency, campaign duration, and daily budget, the answer would be stumbled upon later. It was realized students were already searching for UMSL Day. Summer school, as the result of other marketing channels, was focused on increasing brand awareness. We didn't need to run paid search against these keywords. Meanwhile, non-brand keyword search campaigns for academic programs like nursing, criminology, and master's in business administration were becoming more successful and cost-efficient for finding new students more interested in a particular program than the university's brand.[20]

Of course, UMSL wasn't the only brand studying the effectiveness of brand-keyword searches. The online auction company, eBay, was also conducting research around the same time. Academic researchers in partnership with eBay Research Lab conducted a series of large-scale field experiments to measure the effectiveness of paid search ads, specifically brand-keywords and non-brand keywords. At the time, eBay was bidding on over 100 million keywords and operated search campaigns in 142 Nielsen Designated Market Areas (DMA) across the United States, providing an ideal environment to test. Also the nature of eBay's e-commerce business, they had numerous product categories which varied in competitiveness, market thickness, and general desirability. Meanwhile, a well-known brand allowed them to test both the non-brand keywords for products and the absence of brand-keywords. The research concluded that, in the case of brand-keyword searches, eBay retained 99.5 percent of traffic without paid search ads. It showed that internet users were aware enough of eBay and were going to visit the website regardless, making the brand-keyword search campaigns redundant. While the absence of non-brand ads, eBay traffic dropped forty-one percent and were not regained from organic search.[21] The research from eBay's in this area matched the results UMSL was experiencing with paid brand-keywords. We pulled back spending in that channel, however, in regard to organizations that are small, new, or lack brand awareness. All these should review their own keyword data to determine the relative effectiveness of branded keyword search.

There was plenty of criticism regarding eBay's study and efforts within paid search campaigns, accusing the campaigns of being mismanaged and misusing features, like dynamic keyword insertion resulting in poorly written search ads and results.[22] A few years after the study was published, eBay suffered a significant drop in organic search traffic as well, allegedly as the result of manual action by Google for bad search engine optimization practices.[23] Perhaps it was the protective nature of the search marketing industry to reject the study's findings from eBay. There are more incentives for the agencies, consultants, and subject matter experts in paid search to continue to push for brand-keywords to be paid search ads then to welcome the absence. In the same way, those promoting content as king are ill-suited to view the emergence of data objectively. Instead, they prefer to regulate it to a supporting role.

For marketers not in eBay's position, the distribution of brand-keywords as part of a paid search campaign strategy should come down to a few considerations. First, the overall strength of brand awareness and organic search traffic to the organization's website. Websites already benefiting from strong organic search traffic without running brand-keywords may not find any benefits. Next, the defensive position, as eBay's study noted, states that buying brand-keywords allows the company's brand name to stay out of bidding reach of competing companies.[24] The data supports the likelihood of brand-keyword traffic sources to conversion outcomes, which would be helpful here to improve campaigns.

Finally, combing brand-keywords with non-brand keywords into broad phases may have the impact of suppressing the impressions of competitors who are only bidding on non-brand keywords. This occurs when Google prioritizes the full keyword phrase. They become more relevant, giving a favored position for the keyword ad, as illustrated below (fig. 3.1). Examples could be the brand name with the product category or a university name with a degree that is commonly offered.

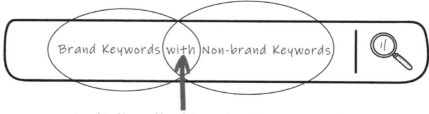

A combined keyword broad phrase that might suppress competition.

Figure 3.1. Illustration by team Charcoal showing Venn diagram combination of brand keywords with non-brand keywords.

Actually, it's Both: the Journey and the Destination

The algorithms that power Google search is the key to how Google has won online search for the majority of the twenty-first century. They are also using location data to transcend into real-world dominance of the new mobile smartphone era. In the same way that Google search wasn't the first search engine; Google Maps wasn't the first online map website. In her article for Recode about the history of Google Maps after its first ten years, Silicon Valley-based business technology reporter Liz Gannes wrote about its early days. Discovered the day before it was supposed to be made public in 2005 by an avid Google watcher and posted on the technology social news website Slashdot, it amazed initial visitors back then being a web application where users could interact with the online map. At the time, it was still a copy-cat product. Other competitors in the space, like Yahoo and MapQuest, were already successful with their online maps. The web application combined satellite data, mobile traffic application, and direction mapping technology. Within two years, it made Google Maps the second most trafficked site after Google search by the end of 2006.[25] However, just having an online map website as part of the search platform isn't what makes location important. Rather, it's the dominance of Google Maps, how mobile smartphones have enabled online discovery in the real world, and how using location extensions in Google Ads enables a marketer to access these data points.

There are two factors that helped power Google Maps' dominance over other location technology. The first was that Google allowed open access for developers to integrate with their websites and mobile applications via a software development kit (SDK) or application programming interface (API), allowing it to gain users and data at an incredible rate. Data from websites monitor technology usage and show that Google Maps and Google Maps API are used by eighty percent of websites that use mapping according to BuiltWith.[26] The API is used ninety-eight percent of the time over competitors according to Stackshare,[27] and with almost a million companies according to iDatalabs.[28] Google Maps was also the original maps application for iPhone's operating system and later Google's own Android. Before Apple created an application and started to compete with Google, they partnered together. When Apple first introduced the iPhone in early 2007, it featured two default applications from Google: YouTube and Maps. Both of these applications were designed by Apple but used Google's SDK for the map's data. Five years later, Apple removed both as default applications. It replaced the data in Maps with their own less superior data sets.[29] Within a few months, Google would release Google Maps onto Apple's iOS ecosystem via Apple's AppStore. Meanwhile, the Android operating system was deployed across numerous smartphone makers each including Motorola, HTC and Samsung. This resulted in an increase in both market share of the mobile operating systems and the usage of Google Map's application which was installed by default.[30] The second factor that has contributed to its dominance is the considerable amount of time and resources Google has spent to keep it beyond rivals. Satellite imagery, street view vehicles recording imagery, and licensing data from third parties for accuracy finally puts these different parts of the puzzle together. Consider that, since 2007, Google has deployed its Street View auto-piloted cars to capture 360-degree imagery across the globe. It has photographed over ten million miles, circling the Earth more than 400 times. Its satellite photos have mapped out parts of the world where ninety-eight percent of people live.[31] Cartographer Justin O'Beirne has studied this market advantage of Google Maps overtime, stating, "Google has gathered so much data, in so many areas, that it's now crunching it together. It's creating features that Apple can't make, surrounding Google Maps with a moat of time."[32] Again, the strength of any platform is both the access to data and users, each improving the results for the platform. By being on all major smartphone operating systems from the beginning, as well as being the website and mobile application developers mapping software of choice, Google Maps has positioned itself as the indispensable location application. Google, then, helps its service maintain its market share by constantly providing it data.

When *Popular Mechanics* listed the "101 Gadgets That Changed The World," the number one item was mobile smartphones. It beat out the lightbulb, the telephone, and all technology that powered the broadcast era like radio and television.[33] Consider for the most part that the mobile smartphone hasn't been in the world nearly as long, and yet, its impact is felt in nearly every corner of the economy. Already, mobile smartphones account for more than half of traffic on the internet.[34] For Gannes, it was obvious that maps would be the killer app for mobile. "The fact that your phone knows where it's located means you can drive yourself somewhere new, find a nearby coffee shop, route around traffic, and hail an Uber."[35] The always-on nature of mobile technology, combined with accurate mapping technology, enabled a new era of ad targeting for marketers with geo-fencing.

With online mapping technology, marketers are able to target the street level with digital ads, allowing for an unparalleled level of accuracy. Wesley Young, vice president of public affair for the Local Search Association, wrote about three types of geo-location focused tactics. The first is geo-fencing enables the marketer to set a perimeter around a physical location, serving both mobile and desktop ads to users in that specific area. Second is geo-conquesting, a variation of geo-fencing, where the perimeter is around a competitor's physical location. It delivers ads to entice consumers towards the marketer's product or service instead. The third is the concept of geo-aware ads that combine real-time location data of the user and serves a location appropriate message. It adjusts for local conditions like season, weather, and events.[36] The advantage of Google's search platform is how all intent, combined with location data, delivers relevant advertising and tracking for marketers. Google's position is that if internet users look for something near them, Google Ads can supply the relevant local search ad or within Google Maps a promoted pin advertisement showing the location. Then, by using store visits as the conversion metric, Google can tell if the ad interaction was followed by a location visit for attribution.[37]

Search Ends with Intent in Mind

Organizations have a lot to consider when choosing platforms. The next two chapters will focus on social and e-commerce. The takeaway for search is understanding intent. Does the product or service benefit from intent-based searching, and if so, how and why should be the focus of marketers when utilizing the platform's advertising options. The abundance of data available on search platforms, including location-based data points, can assist marketers with creating campaigns that use intent as a bridge between users and products or services. Search, however, can't solve for brand awareness. Either the brand keywords are present or only the product or services keywords are. Then, it becomes a matter of positioning within the search advertising space. Nor can it solve for product or service market fit. If the customer doesn't realize they want or need something, they won't know the keywords that will lead them to it. Google Ads offers other channels outside of search, but by themselves, these channels are not as valuable as combing it together with their search platform options.

Content optimizations alone in the hopes of never-ending free website traffic does not meet the reality of finding intent from search platforms. It also misses the insights from audiences that marketers are trying to reach.

These are available in keyword and analytics data, both tools that Google provides organizations to help improve the user experience of ads and websites. Google has effectively left the role of using content as the only vehicle of an organization's brand awareness, driving down a road without a map and blindfolded to the activities of others on the journey. The different forms of keyword data have replaced content as the center of consumer intent in the information era.

To understand intent within the context of search or as it relates to an organization's product or keywords requires data points. More than the data the user provides at sign-up or purchase, intent data is found in analysis of activity whether online or offline. The advantage of gathering these data points regarding intent is the ability to test them within attribution models in order to determine what keywords are successful in a campaign. Prior marketing channels couldn't provide for this type of accountability. If an organization launched a radio campaign across multiple stations resulting in a spike in sales, they wouldn't know which station had the right ones. Marketing pioneer and successful retail merchant John Wanamaker is credited with saying, "Half the money I spend on advertising is wasted; the trouble is I don't know which half."[38] The advantage of advertising on search platforms like Google is that marketers can always see the half that is working when they consider intent.

CHAPTER FOUR

It's a Social World After All

It always felt like I was stuck in my own Groundhog Day. Each media day, I listened to pitches from every radio station, print publisher, and billboard company in St. Louis, who wanted to be part of the media mix for the upcoming year at the UMSL. It wasn't my job to decide who gets what or how much. My role at the meeting was the same as it has been for years, to shoot down the inevitable digital media part of the pitch. At this point, all of the traditional media outlets for radio, billboard, and print would bring their digital media options for their pitch. Gone were the simple offers to run free display banners that added value to their website. The majority were offering targeted display campaigns across digital advertising networks that they were just sure our audience visited daily. But they weren't requesting to place tracking codes on our website to ensure the audience's targeting.

Later, those media outlets associated with a larger media conglomerates and started to have their own in-house digital team to assist with the pitch. Their young digital marketing specialists, tagging along to the meeting, implied the physical manifestation that old media could still be young, hip, and tech driven if given the chance. Still, year after year, it was always new faces in that role. The previous digital marketing guru had moved on, and their LinkedIn connection requests were their only digital legacy.

Again and again, it didn't matter about their digital pitch. The answer was always, "No." I learned early in my experience with digital marketing that the outcome from these stations and publishers were never worth the effort. Once, I agreed to a digital campaign from a print publisher that had built microsites for every high school sports team in the area. It was, in theory, a good fit for UMSL being a more regional university. News, schedules, scores and more content were available. It should be an ideal audience for the university according to the publisher, and we wanted to expand the first-time freshman student population. The publisher also argued that parents would be interested in the microsite's content. And, by knowing the role that parents have in college decisions, we would be reaching both audiences at the same time. It was supposed to be a good deal. And yet, with display ads covering the microsites for over a month, we registered fewer click-thru traffic than fingers on both hands. There were zero conversions for our open house. A valuable lesson learned: don't go where someone tells you the students are, but go where it is proven they are instead.

Facebook Platform

Many organizations and founders likely start with the idea that their product or service will change the world, though few ever achieve any measurable success towards that goal. As the largest social media platform, Facebook can undoubtedly argue they have succeeded in their mission of bringing the world closer together.[1] This accomplishment is achieved by virtue. It reflects the incredible number of users on the platform, how it achieves that size with growth, and the amount of time users spend on the platform. Like other platforms central to the data democracy, Facebook wasn't the first social network nor is it the only social media website that still exists. But its sheer data advantage in many social categories creates a commanding position from which to dominate. If search engines are the way people connect with websites across the internet, then social media networks are the way people connect with each other.

The Global Policy Forum has said that, when large groups of people form strong bonds together as "an imagined community" on a grand scale, they have formed together as a nation.[2] By that standard, Facebook has formed the largest nation on Earth with over 2.5 billion active users[3] as its citizens each month, which is more than the population of the largest real-world nation China (1.4 billion)[4] with another billion people to spare. And yet, Facebook the company owns more than just one social media network.

They own photo-sharing social media network Instagram that has over one billion monthly active users after buying it in 2012.[5] They own messaging mobile application WhatsApp with more than 1.5 billion monthly active users after buying it in 2014.[6] Within the platform is also Messenger. It has become its own mobile application, with another 1.3 billion monthly active users to consider as part of the platform.[7] Why size matters to a social media network is the same how data matters to any platform. The people on this platform have data points that help them connect to other people. This encourages more people to join the platform to make connections, while also helping the platform find more people to connect with each other and so on.

No product or service, whether it is a platform or not, hits a billion users overnight. Even Facebook's beginnings as TheFacebook, exclusive to college campuses across the United States, resulted in less than a hundred million users.[8] Facebook had to develop an explosive growth strategy to become the dominant social platform, or at the very least copy one. LinkedIn, a business and employment-oriented social network, developed a feature called "People You May Know" in 2006. Originally, it displayed its suggested connections as ads that got the highest click-through rate the website had ever seen. Facebook didn't even bother to come up with a different name for it when they released their own version.[9]

"People You May Know" starts at the user sign-up stage. After creating the account with an email address, the user is prompted to connect with people already on the website through a find-people-by-email function. Facebook then keeps all the email addresses from every contact.[10] Users then connect with other users they already know on the network, while inviting those that Facebook didn't have already have a user account with to sign-up. However, the data collection didn't stop with an email address. Instead, users were encouraged to add more data to their profile and make more data available from their address books. Thus, it increased the ways to connect. All this data, in turn, solved the network part of the social equation for the platform. That accumulation of contact data from hundreds of people means that Facebook probably knows every address at which a user has ever lived, every email address they've ever used, every landline and cell phone number with which they've ever been associated, all of their nicknames, any social network profiles associated with the user, all their former instant message accounts, and anything else someone might have added about them in their address books. The company's ability to perceive the threads connecting its two billion-plus users around the globe led it to announce last year that it's not six degrees that separate one person from another, but rather, just three and a half.[11] The person previously in charge of "People You May Know," VP of Engineering at Facebook Lars Backstrom, during a presentation on the feature in July 2010, noted it was responsible for a significant portion of all friending on Facebook. That was important because people with more friends used the website more.[12]

It is not enough for a platform to be incredibly big and always growing with more users unless the users stay and keep coming back. Data from market research company Forrester shows that Facebook dominates the social media usage landscape with fifteen average days per month and eight sessions per day. Meanwhile, Instagram averaged eleven days per month and six sessions per day. Facebook Messenger came in third with almost eight average days per month and three sessions per day. In the same survey, other social media platforms, Twitter, and Google+ significantly averaged fewer days per month and sessions.[13] With users constantly on the platform, their engagement is dependent on both what they share with other users. Moreover, it relies on what they consume from the various social feeds.

Facebook, like any platform, is powered by a complex algorithm that is always changing and improving with data from users. Since 2018, the algorithm's focus has been on favoring "meaningful social interactions" from friends and family. It de-prioritizes content shared by media and businesses.[14] Facebook personalizes each social feed for every user around four data points: inventory, signals, predictions, and score. Inventory includes all the available content on the platform, whether it's posted from friends, family, groups they've joined, or pages they've liked. Signals are the numerous engagement factors liking, sharing, and commenting weighed against what is shared, who shared it, when and what relation to the user. Predictions are where the algorithm considers the user's profile and previous behaviors in an attempt to work out how likely the user will like or interact with content. In this way, it keeps stuff the user won't engage with out of their timeline. The score becomes the value the platform views as relevant to the user. The higher the score, the more likely it appears.[15] Every time a user engages or doesn't interact with content in their feed, it improves the algorithm that is constantly updating based on each new data point the user visits in order to keep their attention on the platform.

Facebook's mission may be to connect the world, but its business model is about audience attention. While the concept of social media platforms is a twenty-first-century invention, the capturing and reselling of attention has been a model of business for centuries. As an author and professor of law, science and technology at Columbia Law School, Tim Wu wrote, "A large number of modern organizations, from posters in late nineteenth-century Paris, through the invention of mass-market newspapers that made their money not through circulation but through ad sales, to the modern industries of advertising and ad-funded radio and television." From Wu's point of view, Facebook is in a long line of such enterprises. Though, it might be the purest ever example of an organization whose business is the capture and sale of attention.[16] The biggest difference is how the attention is cultivated. Previous forms of media were overly reliant on content producers and gatekeepers to create and curate content, while Facebook relies on the user and the algorithm. The previous mass media channels like broadcast-television networks needed programming executives and research teams choosing what viewers watched. Now, algorithm programmers are exclusively responsible. Likewise, everyone with a television and an antenna could see what was on the broadcast networks. Facebook news feeds are personalized, so no one outside or inside the company actually knows what anyone else is seeing.[17]

Move Fast and Break Things

A social media platform started on college campuses and built around connecting friends and family doesn't appear to have a place for organizations. At the beginning for Facebook, it just wasn't a priority compared to user growth. However, in November 2007, they released Facebook Pages as a solution for organizations seeking to reach their audience on the platform.

Pages allowed organizations to engage with users on Facebook by posting content that would appear in user feeds. By 2016, over sixty million organizations had Facebook Pages.[18] Their other platforms Instagram and WhatsApp, meanwhile, make less of a distinction between users and organization accounts.

By creating Pages, Facebook signaled that this was the preferred way for organizations to interact with users and stay on the platform. Organizations were then given an array of Facebook advertising options to grow the "fans" of their page and promote messages to their audience. As Facebook continued to grow in both users and Pages, it became clear to organizations their audiences were on Facebook now. And if they weren't on the platform, their competitor would be. This also weakened the position of the publications and media bundles built around letting advertisers reach an audience. This meant virtually that all of the audiences were in the same place. Media entities and advertisers alike know how to target them from drop-down menus like eighteen-to-twenty-four-year-old men in Maryland who are college football fans. The ads materialize in the feeds of that demographic.[19]

Facebook doesn't require the use of social ads with Pages. Being free for organizations, it almost overnight became a new channel for publications and marketing to distribute content. The hope was that content would go viral, spreading across millions of social feeds without a single dollar for advertising. The mechanism behind this belief was that content would appear as a post in their fans' social feed. The fan, always being super engaged with the organization's page, would engage with the post by liking, commenting, and sharing. Thus, it exposed the organization's content to their friends on the platform. Someone in that user's network then likes the organization's page because they thought the content was engaging. The content viral cycle repeats. The opportunity for free brand awareness and the social media web traffic that might follow opened new flood gates for content marketers, while shutting out of the organic search engine traffic from Google.

The imagined opportunity was really a broken promise to the idea that organizations would always be able to reach their fans on the platform. Above the difficulty and complexity of trying to bend the social feed algorithm to favor Pages over the user's friends and family was Facebook's control of organic social reach. First, the difficulty for content to be rewarded by the algorithm with social media web traffic is shown to be pointless. In hindsight, users weren't reading what they clicked on. Chartbeat CEO Tony Haile, in a study of user behavior across two billion visits across the web, revealed that a stunning fifty-five percent of users spent fewer than fifteen seconds actively on a web page. Even the idea that content engagement would translate into social sharing was marginal. Articles he tracked with social activity had only eight Facebook likes for every 100 visitors. At the same time, publishers that promoted native ad content on their sites to their social audiences saw engagement tumble to one-third of a typical article.[20] If that wasn't enough to convince organizations there wasn't some viral content sharing miracle on any social platform, Facebook came along to remind everyone who was really in charge. In 2012, Facebook restricted the organic reach of content published from Pages to about sixteen percent.

Two years later, organic reach hit just two percent for Pages with more than 500,000 fans. According to Marshall Manson, then managing director at Social@Ogilvy, unofficial Facebook sources were advising community managers to expect it to approach zero in the foreseeable future.[21] Once again, this shows that there is no such thing as a free platform for content to win website traffic. If users never have to pay for a platform, the platforms will not give content from organizations free reach. Someone, somewhere has to pay and it will never be the users.

Stay Focused and Keep Shipping

Success for marketers on Facebook doesn't hinge on artisan-crafted social posts with a lottery ticket's chance of going viral, nor does it require a social media command center that rivals NASA with a 24/7 PR social media engagement team. For marketers, success on Facebook requires a scientific approach to targeting, segmentation, and outcomes. Within the Facebook ads platform, a surreal amount of options for any product or services has gathered a sufficient amount of data intelligence about their audience.

In order to target me on Facebook, for example, a marketer could select an age range of thirty-five to forty-five, the St. Louis DMA, and the male gender. With a modest enough budget, they would likely reach me in over a month or more. But this simple demographic targeting is no better than any other traditional channel like radio or television. This approach ignores the sheer amount of data points the platform has on me and every other user. A marketer user can see for themselves by going to Facebook's "Settings" page and selecting "Ads." From there, a Facebook user can find their ad preferences as the platform understands them at that moment in time. This would include interests across news and entertainment, business and industry, people like celebrities, politicians, musicians, food and drink, technology, hobbies and activities, education, shopping and fashion, sports and outdoors, travel, places and events, family and relationships, lifestyle and culture, and other areas of interests. A Facebook user can also view the advertisers who used a contact list added to the platform. It includes info from the user, advertisers whose website or app the user has used, whom the user has visited with regards to location tracking, and whose ads they've clicked. The preferences will also include a section on user information listing data points and categories that advertisers on Facebook can use to target the user. Now consider the additional data points that are possible to expand upon for better targeting. Using myself as an example again, that could be a range of advertisers. I'm listed under "People who may be interested in switching their mobile network or device," likely because of the mobile device relative age. So, I would be of interest for smartphone makers and cell phone carriers. I'm also under "People who are likely to have used a mobile device for thirteen to eighteen months," which is an easy data point to collect based on how I prefer to access the platform. But I can also be combined with my interest in strategy games to make me a preferred audience for mobile turn-based strategy game developers. I may also need some gift product ideas, considering I have "close friends of women with a Birthday in seven to thirty days." It isn't so much using my profile but rather the profile of my social network. Because it shows my "birthday in May," they may just want to target me so I can treat myself instead.

Marketers should consider what they know about their audience when building targeting into their campaigns. Does the data show their interest weighs more heavily with Star Trek over Star Wars? Is it enough to build a segment around? It doesn't mean content for the campaign should look to include Vulcan memes and Wookie jokes; the data points should only be used to improve targeting for conversions. Remember that even the tiniest interaction with the platform is giving it useful data to build a simulation of the user. With over two billion users, Facebook is uniquely positioned to have a model simulation for one out of every four humans on earth.[22] With these models, meaningful targeting based on data points is more than possible. It should be required for marketing campaigns on the platform.

The two universally limited resources in any marketing department are time and money. If a marketer could build an almost unlimited number of targeted segments with creative on this platform, give them an equal budget and have them fight it out until a single segment emerges victorious with the most conversions. However, a more realistic data-centric approach is needed. Marketers are more likely to encounter the eighty-twenty principle popularized by author Richard Koch when seeking to improve their campaigns.[23] In the beginning, the targeted segments and creative elements of the campaign will find about eighty percent of conversion success will likely come from only about twenty percent of the elements. Data can inform the marketer of which elements in the campaign are working and what efforts are not. The unsuccessful eighty percent of the campaign can be deactivated in favor of devoting more resources to the twenty percent that is performing. The campaign will then reach a ceiling of diminishing returns, where more resources into the remaining twenty percent don't improve results. At this point, data from the entire campaign can be used to generate new segments with creative to test for better outcomes, thereby creating a repeating cycle of optimization.

The whole concept of marketing towards outcomes has dynamically changed on the Facebook platform. While display ad networks and traditional media channels preferred to charge by the impression, whether it actually resulted in marketing outcomes was irrelevant. The marketer had paid to reach the audience that was delivered. If they didn't convert, it wasn't on the medium but instead it was the message. Perhaps the creative content was not hitting the mark or the product didn't have market fit. The marketer paid a CPM, cost per thousand views, for the chance to get in front of people, which is still an option on Facebook. Like other platforms, Facebook includes CPC, cost per click, meaning the marketer only pays for direct user actions at a higher rate. However, because of data, Facebook can offer the chance to pay not just for certain audience size or user actions but an actual marketing outcome, like a sale, an app download, or a newsletter subscription. The rate based on CPA, cost per action. It indicates a once-unimaginable metric offered because the platform is so confident in its understanding of people and their preferences that Facebook can essentially guarantee a certain number of its users will do certain things.[24] By moving the bar on outcomes to a measure for payment, Facebook is putting the money where their audience is as long as the marketer can target the right audience that will most likely to be interested in their product or service. If not, Facebook stops showing the digital ad and displays another organization's campaign that did it right.

Hacker Way

Marketing on Facebook doesn't require a crystal ball-like tool to decipher an organization's audience in order to target them. Where publications or broadcasting were limited by technology in regard to their understanding of audiences, Facebook has no limit with their data. The platform has added to their own data a huge new store of data about offline, real-world behavior, which was acquired through partnerships with other companies such as Experian. It has been monitoring consumer purchases for decades via their relationships with direct marketing firms, credit card companies, and retailers. Experian says its data is based on more than 850 million records of adults, households, and countries. These firms know all there is to know about someone's name and address, their income, level of education, and their relationship status. Plus, they know everywhere they've gone and paid for anything with a card. Facebook can put that identity together with the unique device identifier on each user's phone.[25] More than any other platform, Facebook represents the purest connection between data and users, creating an opportunity for organizations to connect with their audience. This bridge is made possible from a pair of Facebook Ad targeting features called "Custom and Lookalike Audiences." For marketers that have embraced the benefits of a data democracy, these options bring game-changing reach. Meanwhile, marketers with less developed databases are able still to take advantage of a variety of retargeting on the platform in order to start capturing and reaching their audience.

Database marketing didn't start with digital platforms or online in general, but rather in people's mailboxes. That thought for many people likely connected to negative marketing practices like junk mail and its online decedent — spam email. At certain points, every person gets on a list with their data points. It's up to the marketer how best to use it. Many organizations have not done marketing responsibly and have effectively almost ruined channels like direct and electronic mail for the rest. Still, the marketer has his or her database. He or she likely spends time and money keeping it up-to-date only to be confronted with low email open rates and direct mail response. In 2012, Facebook provided that same marketer with a new channel, their platform, to reach the people in their database using Custom Audiences. This targeting feature uses multiple data points like email, a phone number, and other common data points that are legitimately collected. Facebook protects their user data and the marketer's list by matching using a data-security process called hashing, after which the marketer is given a number of users that were matched on the list but will not know who specifically was matched.[26] The significance of adding this targeting feature to the platform allows marketers to reach audiences they are already engaging with directly in other direct channels but with more likelihood of being seen as users spend more time on the platform. Marketers with strong segmented databases can leverage Customer Audiences along the entire consumer journey, delivering relevant creative messages to their audience; more on this in chapters six and seven.

A year after Facebook introduced Custom Audiences, they launched an extension of that targeting option called Lookalike Audiences. It used

Custom Audiences lists as a starting point, while it then looked for data attributes amongst the rest of Facebook users to find people who have similar demographics or interests.[27] With this targeting option, marketers are able to expand their customer data lists from who they know are interested in the product or services to who might also be interested. This feature can be layered with the rest of Facebook's targeting options. Therefore, the potential lookalikes don't go beyond the marketer's main target audiences. The significance this presents to organization can't be understated. This fully leverages the data sets and algorithms that Facebook has on its users to increase reach by significant orders of magnitude.

A Facebook campaign, of which I've discussed in presentations and webinars, uses Lookalike Audiences focused on lead generation for UMSL's open house. We used 300 registrations from the previous open house as the data list. Facebook then found over a million potential lookalikes on the platform. From that total, we segmented down to an audience of over 420,000 potential students living in Missouri and Illinois between the ages of seventeen and twenty-five. If we had stuck with either the total lookalike audience or just the demographics of the audience then the campaign would have overreached, wasting impressions on students unlikely to attend UMSL. The result was that open house registrations increased 306% over five years using Lookalike Audiences. Beyond my experience, Lookalike Audiences (according to AdWeek contributor and director of social media at Yellowhammer Media Group Kirsten Samuelson) have become the "bread and butter" for most Facebook marketers. As a further benefit, in 2017, the platform created more opportunity with Value-Based Lookalike Audiences that uses one additional element from the Custom Audience and CRM data that signifies the value of the customer to the company. As Samuelson points out, customer value can be anything defined by the marketer from lifetime value to total year-to-date sales. Instead of limiting segmentation of this targeting to a small group of valuable customers, with this feature, Facebook has the ability to compare and test against less valuable audiences for an opportunity.[28] This is where the attribution modeling from chapter two can pay dividends for marketers. Analysis can show what types of customers Facebook are more likely to convert for an organization on this platform. Allow media budgeting and creative messaging to be more tailored for each segmentation. For marketers, it also means finding the most valuable data that is essential to building a data democracy. There will be more on this in chapter eight.

Not every marketer has to begin using this platform with a deep understanding of their target audience or customer list by segments. Facebook enables Custom Audiences to be built from website visitors or mobile app users using embedded tracking codes. The barrier of entry is simply having a presence in the digital marketplace. Facebook even lets Custom Audiences be built on engagement with their organization presence across the platform. By beginning with retargeting as a tactic, marketers can leverage the very high likelihood of their customers going to Facebook as one of their billions of users after visiting their organization's website. Facebook has also developed a display network similar to Google to extend advertising, thereby reaching outside their platform. This enables the savvy digital marketer to have a presence and reach. They are able to be inclusive of both search and social platforms but also the available internet for display advertising.

With all the focus on what marketers can get out of the platform and how Facebook empowers that with data, what is missing is the user's value from the advertising. The primary benefit to users from the in-depth targeting related to their data is advertising relevance. Organizations are generally more inclined to target audiences who favor their product or services instead of wasting marketing budgets on groups of disinterested people. Facebook is built around a trade-off that it has asked users to make. It has asked you to provide all your personal information, post all your pictures, tag all your friends, and so on, forever. In return, the platform will optimize your social life.[29] This relationship's stability is positively or negatively impacted by the relevancy of ads, which makes it more important to Facebook that advertisers use the data provided to improve audience targeting. Facebook provides this feedback to marketers in the Ad Manager platform with the Relevance Score that measure several metrics including likes, shares, comments, views, conversions, and negative reviews.[30] The secondary benefit users gain are by the virtue of being a social network in the form of social proof. According to media ratings agency Nielsen, social ads that carry a friend's endorsement generate a fifty-five percent higher ad recall than non-social ads. While ninety-two percent of consumers say they trust recommendations from people they know, seventy percent say they trust consumer opinions posted online.[31] The majority of Facebook ad types allow for users to like, comment, and share in the same way as their personal social media posts. By doing this, they provide organizations additional earned media reach that can extend beyond the paid limits with the potential for endorsement and influence.

The Foolish Wait

Every platform has been forced to adapt to the dominance of mobile smartphones, seeking to bring their same value to users across any device. While Facebook started as a desktop platform accessible through a web browser, smartphones allowed them to build mobile applications to run directly in the operating system. Both Instagram and WhatsApp started as mobile applications, which only later developed desktop web browser parts of their platforms. While Facebook Messenger started within the Facebook platform for desktop web browsers and mobile, they now operate in a sort of hybrid relationship. On the desktop web browser, Messenger is built into the platform experience. Meanwhile, mobile is a separate mobile application. Facebook's mobile strategy has become central to their core mission, so much so that at the end of 2018, mobile advertising revenue was ninety-three percent of all advertising revenue.[32] The platform's mobile focus goes beyond advertising revenue as Facebook holds dominant positions in social login management and messaging.

"Forget your password?" Of course, everyone has at some point. The average person has about 130 online accounts registered to one email address which according to identity management company Dashlane, is a lot to remember.[33] Each account requires password security of varying lengths or complexity. It requires account password reset questions asking about favorite actors, actresses, movies, or pets, and then maybe a mobile phone number to text the user a notification when a password is reset. The absolute worst way to manage that problem is to choose the same password for every account, because if one account system is breached, they all are. Writing each password down, however, runs a different set of risks, and bigger issues in high security organizations. The boom of password management applications presents another solution. Still, every new account requires entering the same information again and again. The alternative to this never-ending struggle from Facebook is a single sign-on social login using a user's profile as both their user account and passkey to third-party sites outside of the platform. Facebook Login gives developers a fast and convenient way for users to create accounts and log into their application, including both major mobile operating systems iOS and Android. Developers get quick account creation, access to profile data for personalization, and social features, allowing them to stay connected off the platform.[34] Facebook gets more data points for their platform because the users are logged into both Facebook and the third-party application at the same time. This strategy has been successful for Facebook to be the social login on desktop or mobile, as it commands the majorities. A 2016 study of social logins by Gigya, a tracking company that provided tools for brands and publishers to let people log into their sites, showed that Facebook had more than sixty percent of market share. With Google in second place at twenty-four percent share of the market, it was trailed by Twitter at seven percent and Yahoo at four percent. Another advantage for Facebook was that it was offered as a social login option nearly 100 percent of the time, along with Google. Conversely, Twitter was only offered seventy-two percent of the time and Yahoo thirty-five percent of the time. More importantly, Facebook was the overwhelming majority on mobile, capturing eighty percent of social logins. This is compared to Google's fourteen percent and Twitter's five percent, while Yahoo registered less than one percentage point.[35] By having an advantage in the mobile market, Facebook is better positioned to offer marketers mobile application install ads than other platforms. Both Google and Facebook have mobile application install ad options across both Apple's iOS and Google's Android. And while both platforms have the ability to track these advertising options to conversion points within the mobile application, Facebook maintains its dominant position in social login. At least as long as it can act as an important way for users to discover new mobile applications, thereby accessing those applications with the user's social profile for login. In this way, they can collect these interactions as data points to improve this process for users and marketers alike.

Business, technology, and media analyst, Ben Thompson, has written extensively on his blog Stratechery regarding Facebook, and its role in the market as an aggregator. He argues that messaging is mobile's killer application. Desktop computers with the internet and a web browser created passive communication. But with mobile smartphones, messaging enables constant communication. What he views as a paradigm shifts in attention.[36] Generally, mobile smartphones have built-in text messaging by way SMS (short message service). More recently, MMS (Multimedia Messaging Service) extends the limitations of carrier bandwidth, extra message data plans, or cross-country capability which opens the door for distribution from mobile applications. While early messaging pioneers like AOL Instant Messenger and Blackberry Messenger saw engagements and adoption from users, neither software moved beyond their initial platforms or devices. Facebook already had messaging as a feature of its platform on desktop and mobile when it purchased WhatsApp in 2014. Strategically the move was defensive. At the time, no single messaging app was more popular than Facebook; however, they were seeing a rise of mobile apps such as WhatsApp, WeChat, Kik, Kakao, Line, and Viber that were together likely collecting more users and sending more messages than just Facebook.[37]

To understand the potential that Facebook sees in this space, you only have to look at Asia, where messaging mobile app WeChat plays an oversized role as a platform. *The Economist* wrote that WeChat acts as the central hub for all internet activity in China. WeChat offers not only messaging, but also group chats, free video calls, file sharing, and more. WeChat includes a payment service that has become almost universally accepted in China. It includes everything from shopping online, paying at physical stores, utility bills, booking and paying for taxis, scheduling deliveries, theatre tickets, and hospital appointments — all without ever leaving the WeChat universe.[38] In order to replicate the same functions outside China, Facebook needs a series of application programming interfaces with a variety of different services. Almost none are tied to a single platform today in the United States or other parts of the globe. While WeChat has not been successful in exporting its platform outside of China, Facebook has already grown. It has created a large user base in India, with an estimated 300 million Facebook users and 200 million WhatsApp users. Since 2018, Facebook has launched its Marketplace feature in India, which lets users to buy and sell items available in their neighborhood. It has further attempted to launch WhatsApp Pay and likely looks to bring its cryptocurrency Libra to the country as well.[39] With WeChat, Facebook knows what is possible with messaging as a platform. It also knows how that integration fits into the daily lives of its users. Marketers have already started to embrace messaging in terms of engagement with customers. Offering chatbots automates this effort at scale for products or services. The long game for organizations in this space is the development and integration of services into messaging platforms, including payment features. Until then, Facebook already offers Facebook Messenger ads to grow those inevitable channels for users.

Our Work is Never Over

Whether the future of Facebook is in messaging, its success as a social media platform should not only be measured by its size and revenue but the number of social media networks it has sent to a digital graveyard. Consider the networks that launched successfully before it like Friendster and MySpace, which are defunct or irrelevant. The networks that tried to carve out a niche space in music like Apple's iTunes Ping or Path limited users to fewer friends for more personal interactions. Now, both are shuttered. Even Google tried and failed in social with Google+ despite its advantage in user data from search. It, too, was shut down in 2019. Hundreds, if not thousands of networks, have come at them only to miss. As long as people prefer to use Facebook more than anything else, it will continue to dominate. At this point, technology reporter Charlie Warzel, wrote, "Facebook is intimidatingly large and deeply woven into our cultural fabric, largely because we have allowed it to become so. We can't consider a world without Facebook in it."[40] So, this might be Facebook's world now and we are just living in it!

There will continue to be examples of social media content that goes viral and spreads across hundreds of millions of news feeds on this platform. Every Make-A-Wish kid that gets to be Batkid for the day gets to ride around San Francisco in the bat mobile, fighting crime while generating 1.8 billion social impressions,[41] just as the ALS Association's Ice Bucket Challenge that involves celebrities and everyday people. In total, it raised $115 million in the summer of 2014[42] for a good cause. There follows hundreds of copy-cat efforts that fail and how-to articles giving advice on how to replicate the success of these campaigns that will fall short. Because, not every product or service category has the potential ability to go viral. Facebook has made sure to limit the chances of those that try, fearing that it would overwhelm user centric content. This means there is no formula on social media that guarantees marketing content will go viral. Organizations should always be wary of third parties that promise it will. Only they know how to find success on the platform with content.

There is no secret sauce for success on Facebook. The data that is available on their over 2.5 billion users is the same for every organization, large and small. The more an organization understands about their consumers, the more they stand to gain over their competitors. For marketers tasked with building audiences, from brand awareness to lead generation, this platform gives them the ability to start from no one to everyone. Organizations that have already created their data democracies can take advantage of Facebook's scale with billions of possibilities made possible only by data.

CHAPTER FIVE

The Everything You Didn't Know You Needed Store

It must be a universal fate of parents to tell their children at least once, that back in their day, it was harder to accomplish something than it is today. I know my parents said it to me more than once in my childhood. I found myself recently saying it to my young son one evening before bed. His mother had ordered the next book in the *A Series of Unfortunate Events* series for him from Amazon. In his mind, waiting two days for the free Prime shipping felt like forever, at which point the voice that all dads have kicked in for me, "Back in my day, we ordered from the Sears Catalog. It took weeks to arrive, and you went to the store to pick it up. You have no idea what waiting means," I said. I'm sure my righteous indignation with him registered, the same way it did with me at his age with internal eye-rolling. My parents likely did the same with their parents, all the way back to some Homo Sapien child complaining about how the fire wasn't warming the cave fast enough.

Even today I still remember experiencing the pure bliss while reading the Sears Catalog and making my wish list for Santa. I'm not sure how my parents had persuaded me that Santa preferred me to go into the Sears Catalog and mark what I wanted for the holidays. I'm not even sure that, somewhere along the way, I hadn't convinced myself it was all part of Santa's grand plan. There just wasn't enough time to go to every child's house in the world on Christmas Eve. That was why I figured he worked with Sears to deliver children's gifts to their stores instead. Parents picked up the gifts, wrapped them, and made sure they were under the tree by Christmas. At whatever point, this grand illusion was shattered. It made no difference to me, since the Sears catalog continued to play an outsized role in my holiday gift selection for several years to follow.

At one point in time, Sears was considered a game-changer in retail. In the early 1900s, the United States population lived in rural areas. They bought almost everything from the general store in town. Then along came the Sears Catalog, which was delivered to the doorsteps of American homes. According to Bloomberg writer Kim Bhasin, it fundamentally changed how people shopped in United States. The small-town general store had a limited selection and charged exorbitant prices because they were the only game in town. The Sears Catalog provided shoppers more choice than ever before, and at lower prices.[1] In the decades that would follow, Sears would become a cornerstone of the American shopping mall experience, moving the focus from rural areas to urban centers. They opened several hundred stores, and diversified its offerings to include major national brands, insurance, real estate, and financial services. However, even a merger with big box department store chain Kmart couldn't hold off the distribution of the internet era. E-commerce stores became the new catalog without the limits of printed pages or costs to maintain multiple physical stores near consumers. By 2018, Sears Holding filed for Chapter 11, and auctioned off at a bankruptcy court that year.[2]

The Everything Platform

The virtually endless marketplace analogy that began in chapter one comes full circle when looking at the final platform of this book — the e-commerce giant of Amazon. For other platforms in this book, the connection between what they do for their users, such as providing internet search results or a social network of family and friends, does not directly create the revenue that has helped make them dominate. Instead, those platforms used advertising placed within their platform to produce revenue. And yet for Amazon, that connection is direct. From the beginning, they have sold products to consumers as the main function of their platform. The addition of advertising to their platform for marketers, much later, was simply a value add in order to sell more products to consumers.

The self-proclaimed everything store offers just about anything that can be sold legally on the internet, delivering to a user's mailing address. It started in just one product category, books, in 1994. From there, Amazon expanded its offerings into more media categories like music CDs and DVD movies. As of 2019, it has expanded to almost 120 million products across multiple categories.[3] It isn't enough of an advantage that Amazon offers so many products, because alternative e-commerce sites are always one click away. So, they also need a pricing advantage. However, neither all the products nor the lowest price can create a platform advantage without data. Here, one of Amazon's many algorithms creates dynamic pricing where the prices of products are changed millions of times per day. With this strategy, they reportedly take into account user intent, product demand, and pricing patterns from other retailers.[4] This is not Amazon's only algorithm nor its only advantages over other e-commerce sites or offline retailers.

Amazon being the biggest or the cheapest isn't what makes it the dominant e-commerce platform. Like all platforms, Amazon uses data for the improvement of user experience, from beginning to end. It's their focus on improving that experience that puts them at the center of the e-commerce experience on the web. While other platforms have user accounts, Amazon takes it one step further with a membership program called Prime. It delivers increasing value, based on repeat purchasing. Finally, as the saying goes, Rome wasn't built in a day. It is also true for Amazon, but it also wasn't alone in building its e-commerce empire either. After all, Amazon enlists third-party sellers in the Amazon Marketplace to list and sell their products from within the platform. From this high-ground position, Amazon is able to leverage these advantages back to brands. As a result, their marketers make them the biggest threat to all other platforms.

It's All About the Long Term

When you look at thousands of different e-commerce sites across hundreds of different product categories, the one thing they might have in common is that they're all different when it comes to laying out their content for each product. Amazon, however, has one kind of page for all of its products across its site. From their point of view, the role of content is to be consistent. Amazon did this from the start, only making improvements to their product page while never allowing inconsistency between product pages. Unlike the prior two platforms in this book, there was no great betrayal from their algorithms or false broken promises against organizations featured on Amazon's platform. Amazon was able to do this because of their control of content and because of this consistency. Even when they allowed third parties on the platform with Amazon Marketplace, each seller had to be consistent with their content within Amazon's product webpages. Because of that, it is hard to tell when you are not buying directly from Amazon. And, that is the point. Perhaps the scariest part of Amazon to other organizations is when their empire moves into new products or service categories. They dominate it, and then make every organization in those categories rely more on Amazon for the majority of its sales.

These content rules, however, don't apply to Amazon. Once they started to create products for themselves, their product pages featured better content with different layouts. As an example, when looking at both their Echo[5] smart-speaker and Kindle[6] e-reader compared to other smart-speakers[7] and e-readers[8], users will find several differences. For starters, Amazon adds a banner at the top of only their own products that shows how it is part of their product line. Other product pages include "Sponsored Products Related to This Item" and "Customers also Shopped for..." carousels of other products. Meanwhile, Amazon products go straight to the feature section. When the user reaches the "Compare with Similar Items" section, Amazon only compares its products to other Amazon products. All the while, other product pages include competitors in their lists. The advantage to Amazon is being able to showcase more about their product with less competition from similar products on their platform. These types of features aren't unique to Amazon, as other e-commerce websites and retailers have created their own generic products or services to favor themselves over other brands.

The purpose of e-commerce sites is to sell, of course, so it would be counterintuitive to include content that discourages a transaction. Platforms, however, focus more on user experience. With that in mind, Amazon includes customer reviews on all of its product pages. Amazon does not cherry pick these testimonial reviews, but rather includes both positive and negative reviews on a five-point star scale. The importance of good reviews is obvious in that it encourages purchasing of that product, while negative reviews that might discourage a transaction can be viewed more from the lens preventing unsatisfied user purchases. Thus, it keeps that user coming back to the platform for future transactions.

Amazon works hard to maintain the integrity of their product review system on the platform. They routinely monitor for fake reviews and abuses of the system by sellers or brands. While highlighting actual reviews from transactions on the platform, they mark those reviews as verified purchases. Amazon also encourages its users to be prolific reviewers. Users are encouraged to create a list of top reviewers on their platform, a reviewer Hall of Fame[9], and Vine an invite-only review perk program.[10] By creating a community of reviewers, Amazon has developed a perpetual engine of product feedback for its users, showing what customers like them have also bought. Each becomes a data point contributing to an improved experience on the platform.

During an interview in 1999, founder Jeff Bezos said, "If there is one thing Amazon.com is about, it is obsessive attention to the customer experience, end-to-end."[11] Perhaps one of the most critical parts of that experience on the platform is search. Whereas Google focused on offering search across the entire internet, Amazon's focus is always on Amazon. A standard navigation menu dependent on mouse clicks would be insufficient to manage hundreds of millions of products. It would mean possibly dozens of clicks to just reach the right product. A pure transaction intent-based search, however, provides frictionless browsing. The search algorithm is secret, of course, but there are a few factors that affect search product result pages. According to Amazon product research tool Jungle Scout, this includes a sale velocity of how often a sale occurs and sale profit. Conversion rates and relevancy to the search request are compared to other products of the same keywords. Along with variety, even the best-selling product with a category should have options for users to compare.[12] While search engines for the internet have the limitation of only being able to optimize search results and not the actual content of the web, Amazon's advantage is that their search is for their e-commerce platform. So, they can optimize both the results and the product pages. Users have responded positively to this strategy. A research study by Feedvisor on consumer behavior showed that Amazon was the "go-to destination for search and purchase." The majority of people started their search for new products on the platform. When they were ready to buy, they returned again for the purchase.[13]

Obsessing Over Customers

Retail membership programs did not begin with Amazon Prime. They were neither the first, nor likely the first on the Internet. But arguably, since they began in 2005, they have become the most successful with over 100 million members.[14] The Amazon Prime Program delivers value to its members in many different ways: from unlimited video streaming from Prime Video of award-winning shows competing against Netflix and Hulu, to offering Amazon Prime Music - an ad-free music streaming service with over two million songs. It competes against Spotify, Pandora, and Apple Music. Unlimited photo storage competes against a plethora of options including Google Photos and Yahoo! Flickr. Amazon even started a members-only Prime Day sales event in 2015. By 2018, it was the biggest sales event day for the platform, and in total, it ranks fourth for online holiday shopping. It competes with internet-wide holidays Singles Day, Cyber Monday, and Black Friday.[15]

The above-mentioned benefits of the membership program have just been additions over the years. The original and most important value is free two-day shipping for purchases on the platform. The reason why this makes the biggest difference and provides the most value is that Amazon can make the prices on its platform. This factor can add cost and cause delay, compared to other e-commerce websites is shipping. By removing this factor and transferring the cost to the membership program, it reduces the likelihood the user will go to another e-commerce website to make the same purchase where it isn't free. This also has an impact against offline competitors, as well as when the only remaining benefit for a purchase at retail stores is that the product is made available to them on the same day. Though, Amazon can negate this by having less overhead cost absent physical locations near all their customers. Amazon is also working to close this gap as well. According to Alison Griswold, business reporter for Quartz, the platform's new goal is to evolve the two-day free shipping program into a one-day free shipping program. The company believes one-day shipping could help it bring in the next wave of new customers.[16] This allows them to remain competitive with price and to provide value over the long term with the program, even to the point of showing members how much they have saved on shipping from all purchases during the membership. In theory, this fuels the repeat purchasing cycle. There is data that supports this behavior as well. A research study by Feedvisor showed that ninety-six percent of Prime members are more likely to buy products from Amazon than other e-commerce websites. They are also more likely to be daily or almost every day purchases by eighty-nine percent. And, Prime-eligible products are seventy-five percent more likely to be considered by members when searching on the platform.[17]

This is important to organizations when considering e-commerce strategies for their products, especially if they are considering making that product available on Amazon and eligible for Prime shipping with purchase. It is not the only factor that should be considered. Although, the dominance of the platform with the transactional part of the internet means they can't be ignored either. Consider that, according to analysts at Macquarie Research, Amazon takes twenty-four cents of every one dollar of retail sales. But, it also takes fifty-one cents of every one dollar in sales for only online retail purchases.[18] This is why having data points related to a consumer's journey are critical starting points in a data democracy.

The Infinite Looping Marketplace

Again and again, major platforms have turned to other organizations to help them expand in exchange for access to their audience that they've built. In Amazon's case, it was the addition of third-party sellers in 2006 under the Marketplace program. Both shared that access and expanded its product offerings. There is a good chance that, when buying something from the platform today, consumers aren't buying from Amazon directly. Instead, customers are buying from one of six million sellers. Behind any item for sale, there could be dozens of sellers, all competing for the same click. Marketplace sales were almost double those for Amazon, directly making the third-party sellers on the platform alone the larger e-commerce business.[19] The immediate advantage to Amazon and its users is that the third-party sellers offer scale for both more products and more suppliers for products, essentially driving down cost. Third-party sellers get access to millions of users that they didn't have to find, attract, or maintain a self-sufficient e-commerce website to compete against Amazon for those same users.

Amazon offers more than any other platform when it comes to access for organizations on that platform. On Google and Facebook, access to the audience of users and advertising to those users is the limit. For Amazon, organizations can use the very same infrastructure the company has created to service its Prime members. Amazon Fulfillment options allow organizations, for a fee, to ship their product to an Amazon warehouse, after which Amazon handles all distribution, shipping, and customer service.[20] Other companies can offer brands fulfillment-as-a-service for their products, but only Amazon can make that product available for Prime shipping. Because growing Prime membership is central to Amazon's strategy, their Prime users prefer products with prime shipping. After all, it creates an infinite preference loop within their consumer journey that creates an advantage for product sellers.

This loop, sometimes called the Amazon Flywheel, is internally referred to in the company as the Virtuous Cycle and even has its own origin story. According to Jeffrey Wilke, Amazon's CEO of Worldwide Consumer in an undated YouTube video titled "*Virtuous Cycle*"[21] and author Brad Stone from his book *The Everything Store,*[22] the Virtuous Cycle was written by founder Jeff Bezos at a company offsite back in 2001 on a napkin. Both explain that Amazon's superior customer experience leads to more website traffic. More customers increases the volume of sales, which attracts more third-party sellers to the site, which in turn, increases selection. The more sellers use Amazon for fulfillment services, it allows the platform to get more value from fixed costs like their warehouses and web servers. More efficiency allows for lower prices on the larger selection or products, looping the cycle back to improving the customer experience. Finally, if any part of the flywheel was increased, it would accelerate the whole loop. Both

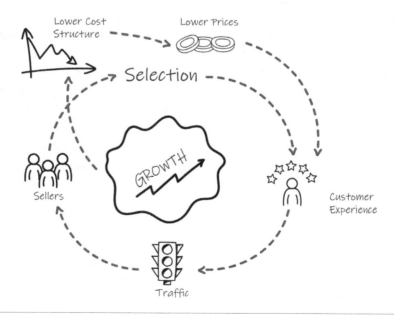

Figure 5.1. Illustrations by team Charcoal of Virtuous Cycle. Wilke, Jeffrey. Virtuous Cycle. Accessed December 6, 2019. https://www.youtube.com/watch?v=5jcDlGn-tZA.

Amazon and its users benefit by increases, while sellers only benefit when their product is purchased. The Virtuous Cycle, however, overlooks how marketers for third-party sellers and brands with products on the platform can accelerate the loop to their benefit with advertising.

From A to Z to Threat

Marketers with products on Amazon face many of the same challenges as they would on Google or Facebook. Sure, that product might benefit from the platform's algorithms or its brand awareness, generating a steady stream of sales. At the same time, other products benefit from just Prime availability. Strong user review feedback wins categories for search result pages. The reality for the remaining millions of products and new entrants on the platform is how to stand out and get attention. By virtue of being both the last platform featured and the last to develop advertising for marketers, much of Amazon's two options will be familiar. Sponsored product search ads are based on keywords like Google, to native display product ads based off interests or similar products, and off platform retargeting like Facebook. Similarities aside, its impact is already being felt with revenues increasing by 250 percent in 2018 compared to 2017. It has brought Amazon into third place for digital advertising revenues for the first time. Some industry experts predict that the long-standing advertising duopoly of Google and Facebook will turn into a triopoly as soon as 2019. Then, Amazon will be charging right behind these established incumbents.[23] Amazon represents the biggest threat to the other two platforms they have ever faced, because keywords and the search process is part of the Amazon platform. Therefore, it can siphon search advertising for products from Google. And while Facebook has a tremendous collection of data points, they lack the last piece of the puzzle. The purchase point of products normally occurs off their platform.

The first requirement of Amazon's search advertising options requires that marketers have a product available on the platform. From there, it is a recognizable bundle of features. It includes targeting based on a broad, phrase, and exact keywords with negative keywords to exclude. Keywords can be selected manually or created automatically then cost-per-click bidding within a daily budget. Perhaps it's unfair to label Amazon's search advertising options as a knock-off of Google. Google has to deal with the entire chaos that is the internet, from every single way web pages can be coded, content organized, and information navigable. There are so many variables that Google's algorithm and search platform that the internet has to constantly take into account. Amazon is the opposite in that it deals with the controlled order of its own platform. Every product page has the same setup on the same infrastructure, and within the same data points. All are part of Amazon. They never lose visibility of any part of the search or buying process. Conversely, there are parts of the internet into which Google cannot see or follow a user.

It would be a mistake to view Amazon's search intent as purely transactional either, that users are only looking to complete the purchase of a product from start to finish. There is still very much an informational discovery aspect to search on Amazon. The user may not know everything about the product for which they are looking, which companies make it, or what other users think of that product. So, from a marketer's standpoint, much of the same considerations in terms of keyboard targeting are in play when it comes to understanding search intent. This is more so relevant when considering that about seventy percent of searches on Amazon are for non-branded keyword terms, rather than brand keywords. Because Amazon users prefer Prime, they often purchase the first thing with that shipping option. Marketers could take advantage of positioning on search result pages, out-selling even household names.[24]

Perhaps the biggest advantage for marketers using Amazon's sponsored search is the impact that conversion sales have on products overall position of that product organically. On Google, conversions for search advertising haven't any impact on the relevancy of the search advertisements, to the keywords, or to the organic website rankings. However, Amazon's conversions can play a bigger factor in impacting the organic search ranking of products. According to Andrew Ruegger, managing partner and head of e-commerce & Data Science at GroupM, "The more you sell, the more free marketing Amazon will give you because you are moving units."[25] When considering and testing search ads on Amazon, two data points should be considered by marketers. First, before campaign launch, determine the threshold for the average cost of sales (ACoS) of the product, which is the total ad spend divided by the sales. This is a figure that Amazon campaigns are able to track because the transaction and the campaign occur on the same platform. Compared to the ACoS percentage, the data related to profit per unit will determine if the campaign is a win or loss in terms of return on investment. Second, while running a campaign, the option to have Amazon automatically select keywords for a product is counter to having an intent-based focus. It can be used to take advantage of the platform's algorithm. Marketers should bifurcate their campaign setup into a manual keyword campaign and an automatic keyword campaign. Then, compare converting and non-converting keyword phrases between campaigns. This tactic uses the power of the platform's algorithm combined with the marketer's intent-based keyword data points to have the best of both worlds of machine-learning and human understanding.

Amazon's advertising isn't limited to just search results either. The platform includes display ads conveniently called Amazon Product Display Ads on both category pages and product pages. The ads can appear both in a standalone location or amongst other suggested products based on that product page, unless it's an Amazon product. However, viewing this ad format as simply as another form of web advertising undervalues its target capabilities and data points available. This advertising option includes two targeting options: product targeting and interest targeting. The most direct method, product targeting, allows marketers to directly select the products where they want advertisements to display.[26] With this advertising, vertical marketers can find themselves promoting their products in a way completely unique to this platform, by having advertising appear on the product pages of competitor products. With interest targeting Amazon goes beyond search data, to perhaps their best data points on user buyer behaviors and interests. The very nature of Amazon as an e-commerce platform gives them the distinct advantage against all others, because buying behavior is a primary data point it can track with users. This allows Amazon to provide that type of targeting option, which would otherwise be unavailable to marketers. It allows the platform to connect the dots between similar products purchased, similar interests and different types of product categories. At the same time, these data sets might not be available to the average organization especially if those connections are with products or interests that they don't offer or haven't considered. By having this option, Amazon is setting itself apart from any other type of platform. Amazon keeps this part of their data points closed off from marketers directly but available for targeting, which is not unusual. Facebook does the same thing with custom audiences and likely audiences, not allowing marketers to understand the connecting data points but still benefit from the targeting that the platform has found on their behalf. So, the marketer is able to benefit purely from the algorithm's data learning that the Amazon platform offers without the complexity of having to create those connections.

With both search and display advertising, marketers have powerful options for reaching Amazon's users when they are on the platform. However, Amazon does not limit itself to advertising options that only appear on its e-commerce platform. Marketers can use inbound advertising to drive users to their products on Amazon, while outbound advertising follows users across the rest of the internet, and other sites owned by Amazon. With these options, brands can extend both reach and effectiveness, allowing marketers to go beyond pushing just the product. Rather, they can be pulled with persuasive advertising.

Amazon labels its inbound option as native advertising, which allows for the integration of recommendation ads, search ads, and custom ad types into an organization's website. Recommendation ads work similar to recommendation suggestions on the platform, dynamically showing a product listing based on the product page and its visitor. Search ads operate as an embedded search function showing results based on keywords. Meanwhile, custom ads allow marketers to select products they would like to promote.[27] Inbound is ideal for organizations that don't operate an e-commerce website, while at the same time, it sends users to a platform where they are more likely to have an account for purchasing already, hopefully a Prime membership and a better consumer's experience.

From an outbound perspective, Amazon offers retargeting advertising as an option for its sponsored product ad types. More of a targeting extension than a separate advertising type, this is similar to other platforms in that the advertising will follow users across other websites. The difference is that Amazon's retargeting has more dynamic potential because it can be based on search and consumer behavior from the platform. Normal digital retargeting campaigns can only show the same pair of shoes, for example, over and over again until you purchase them or fall out of the days since the last visit window of the campaign. Meanwhile, Amazon can combine past purchases to show advertising users who are more likely to respond to products based on a certain time of day or season, such as searching for warm weather items in the fall, in anticipation of a vacation trip to the beach. Marketers can send ads matching that product category in anticipation of that journey.[28] All digital marketing campaigns can benefit from retargeting advertising, since it continues to target the consumer's journey. Hence, it does not rely on one platform or one advertisement to result in a conversion.

If there is one thing that conquerors in history and business crave, it's new territory. Amazon, like other platforms in previous chapters, is no different. It has acquired or created a vast amount of companies, services, and websites. Some of these properties like Amazon Web Services, Amazon's publishing arm, audiobook website Audible, and book review website Goodreads were business extensions and acquisitions that feed the Virtuous Cycle for product discovery of their selection or lowering cost structures. While operating, after the acquisition of series of other e-commerce websites, which are niche in focus, but competitive with the main platform, nonetheless, including Zappos (shoes), Shopbop (high-end women's clothing), East Dane (men's clothing), 6pm (discount clothing), Fabric.com (fabric), and Woot! (daily deals).[29] Organizations benefit more specifically from Amazon's booming video business that includes IMDb, Twitch, Prime Videos live sports, and Fire TV devices. Marketers can target these with video ads. IMDb, the acronym for the Internet Movie Database, is the 48th largest website according to Alexa (another Amazon acquisition), which includes just about everything a person needs to know about entertainment movies and television since its inception. In fact, it has likely participated in more games of "Six Degrees of Kevin Bacon" or trivia nights than any other website. Popular video live-streaming platform Twitch might have been seen as a strange territory to acquire back in 2014, for it was a defensive move against Google's YouTube juggernaut perhaps. Now, though, it is an offensive powerhouse. Catering largely to video gamers allows them to both watch and participate in video games as broadcasters, with about fifteen million views each day and 2.2 million streamers. In early 2018, peak concurrent viewership on Twitch was about two million, which is higher than television network audiences of MSNBC, CNN, and Fox News as well as the sports network ESPN at 1.5 million.[30] Live sports has also started to become a new part of Amazon's Prime Video offerings with NFL's Thursday Night Football, British rights for tennis ATP World Tour and US Open on the platform since 2018. Each is built-in advertising breaks. Finally, if that wasn't enough, Amazon also includes video ads on their Fire TV digital media player and Fire tablets devices, each with several tens of millions of users.

In just a few short years of offering advertising products, Amazon already has a lot to offer marketers. Yet, it has the most to grow in the competitive landscape of platforms. Google and Facebook are primarily driven by advertising revenue, while the nature of Amazon's e-commerce focus gives them more incentive to improve the impact advertising has on its users. Perhaps Prime users can benefit from sponsored brands or engagement that enhances advertising deliverability, reach, and effectiveness. It is more important to Amazon that the role of advertising is more supportive of the customer experience without creating any friction that slows growth.

New and Improved Virtuous Cycle

When looking again at Amazon's Virtuous Cycle, marketing from sellers doesn't have a role for increasing growth. The absence of marketing can be explained in that the cycle was created before Amazon introduced advertising on their platform. Any consideration in adding advertising to the Virtuous Cycle model should benefit all parties involved in the process. For Amazon, this means advertising has to power growth, while for users it must improve the customer experience. For sellers, it must be an increase of traffic that results in product sales. Advertising options are based on combinations of customer buyer behavior with data from either search, browsing, or previous purchases. As a result, more relevant ads are possible to improve customer experience. The more relevant the advertisement to the customer, the more likely the advertisement leads to traffic to the seller's product pages. The resulting sales from that traffic gives more opportunity for the seller to be successful on the platform. Thus, they can continue with the rest of the cycle. The growth from the new advertising enhanced Virtuous Cycle comes from two directions (fig. 5.2). The first is by having the data from existing growth on the platform Amazon can enable relevant advertisement for sellers. The second is that the resulting traffic for the seller products on the platform from advertising creates more data that loops back into growth feeding the cycle.

There are several ways indirectly that the advertising enhanced Virtuous Cycle helps expand the platform across the cycle. Organizations that find success from advertising on the platform are more encouraged to expand their selection as sellers. Those competing against the seller off the platform may see an opportunity to join the Amazon Marketplace in order to make their products available for Prime. They may also use advertising to gain traffic for product sales or lower prices to gain favor with the algorithms. Those sellers already competing on the platform that see sales dropping may also drop prices or start using advertising. Both benefit Amazon. Customers on the platform continue to benefit from more selection and prices. Amazon does not have to make a penny from advertisements if it funnels the revenue and data to further growth along the cycle.

Already an ecosystem of third-party services has emerged to provide sellers with resources and expertise to improve their role in the cycle. This includes the optimization of their advertising campaigns. Organizations that have figured out the advantages of Amazon's platform have started to shift. Michelle Castillo of CNBC has reported that an executive from a large advertising agency said, "Some brands find Google search ads quaint and want their budgets moved to Amazon because it directly correlates to sales."[31] This activity feeds both the expansion of successful sellers and improves the platform experience for the consumer. The more that Amazon is used to find anything for which users are looking, the more likely the chance that Amazon will have everything they are looking to buy.

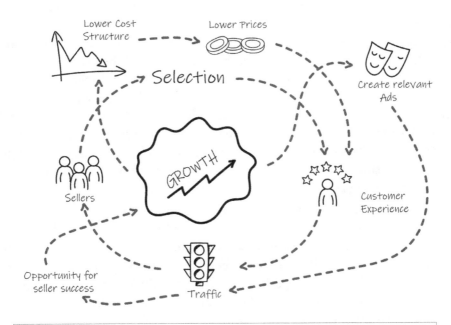

Figure 5.2. Illustrations by team Charcoal of Advertising Enhanced Virtuous Cycle

"Alexa, Send Me an Easy Button"

While Google seeks to bridge the gap between online activity and offline location, Facebook seeks to redefine how we communicate with each other and organizations through messaging. Amazon is already working on ways to reduce or eliminate barriers in the customer experience. Barriers have existed since the beginning of commerce. First, it was the availability of a general store near rural customers. Then, it was catalogs and nation-wide post office networks for delivery. As populations grew, general stores became retail malls and shopping centers with more variety and proximity. Next came online shopping, limitless selection, and fast, cheap delivery methods. At each level, there are barriers within the interactions that had to be solved. What followed from the selection at the general store, were waiting periods on ordering and shipping from catalogs. Next, there was large crowds and checkout lines at retail malls during the holidays. Now, it is the process of selection from the endless virtual marketplace. As writer Amanda Mull explains in *The Atlantic*, when you type hangers into Amazon's search box, the mega-retailer delivers "over 200,000" options. Even if you have very specific hanger needs and preferences, there's no obvious choice. There are just choices. The phenomenon repeats for almost all of the everyday objects Amazon carries: phone chargers, water bottles, flat-panel televisions. And it's not just Amazon.[32] In order to be the platform that removes this barrier of overwhelming choices, Amazon knows it needs to be more easily placed in the consumer's journey. So, it removes the anxiety created by screens filled with endless options. The two ways in which the platform seeks to accomplish this is with smart devices powered by the Alexa virtual voice assistant and Amazon Dash Replenishment Service.

With Alexa, users are able to interact with the platform by simply using their voice. They, of course, realize that just having a device which only takes Amazon orders is simply not enough. In the same way that the internet and mobile devices have opened up new experiences, Amazon has designed the Alexa experience to be more than just the platform. It allows developers to integrate their application and their smart devices with a voice assistant like an operating system. With these integrations, many of the same popular apps and services that have been created in the internet era are available in an Alexa-powered device. It is like the ability to be able to do music streaming, but not just from Amazon's music service. The same occurs with video streaming and smart televisions, not just from Amazon Prime video selection but other services as well. The ability to act as a hub for smartphone lights, thermostats, and hundreds of other devices from other manufacturers takes place with just their voice. By not limiting these devices or the apps and services to only things that Amazon creates, it avoids the wall-garden approach. It expands the circle of consumers interested in becoming users, and developers interested in reaching those users through Alexa. Each new smart device a user owns, along with each new application or order they make expands the data points that Amazon is able to draw upon to offer better products. How this reduces barriers is that, by simply asking for it to buy a household product category, Alexa will provide algorithm-determined options along with the price. This skips the search result page for that product keyword. It further skips the product page, and user reviews. Only if the user doesn't select the limited option are they referred to the Alexa application for additional choices.

The product winners in voice-assisted shopping is whoever the algorithm determines, while the loser potentially is brands. As Scott Galloway, a clinical professor of marketing at New York University Stern School of Business, author, and entrepreneur, points out, the decline of brand began with Google. Every day, fewer people put a brand's name before the product or service keywords in a Google search. According to Galloway, the same is going to happen with voice commands as non-brand usage increases. "The death of brand is here. It has a voice, specifically Alexa." Galloway said in his "Winners & Losers" video series that, while demonstrating how Alexa responded to a voice search for "buy batteries," it provided Amazon generic batteries as the first and second option before sending the user to the Alexa smartphone application.[33] This reduction in choice benefits Amazon either way, since more purchases are made from Alexa. It only benefits organizations when their products are available on the platform and preferred by users.

The platform's second breakthrough in reducing barriers allows smart devices to automatically reorder with Amazon Dash Replenishment Service (DRS). With these, products that require supplies can order from the platform on behalf of the user and will ship to their address. Amazon DRS's enabled printer can sense low ink and reorder print cartridges, a washing machine can monitor detergent use and order more pods, or even batteries for a smoke detector that might save lives. The combinations for devices and their supplies are endless. It is not limited to only supplies from the device manufacturer either. The challenge becomes having to remember when supplies are low or running the risk of being out of something at a crucial point. But with Amazon DRS, its users don't have to remember. For the manufacturers, integration comes at no cost, while product consumption and usage data points are available to both them and Amazon.

If a Head is Cut Off, Two More Shall Take its Place

Today, Amazon is more than a website that sells books. It is a platform with hundreds of thousands of product categories for everything imaginable. Amazon is also more than an e-commerce platform that sells only products. They also sell their services like cloud computing, book publishing, entertainment media, smart devices, live-streaming, retail outlets, a transportation fleet, fulfillment warehouses, and even healthcare technology. These offer more to consumers and organizations, while providing Amazon data insights about their entire virtuous cycle. In none of these areas is Amazon without competition from both big and small organizations. The difference is, however, that Amazon can risk losing revenue along any part of its platform or company if the future outcome is growth.

Content does have a role to play on Amazon for every product, but the reality for the marketer is how their content can be the deciding factor with regards to the millions of different products on Amazon. That is, of course, when their content isn't the factor that is being considered. The algorithm on Amazon is parsing user reviews. Prime shipping availability, and price elasticity are some of the major data points of which the marketer has little control, if any. The algorithm makes the content irrelevant to what is appearing in the search results. Products that Amazon makes themselves don't follow these restrictions, since they have more content freedom and no competition on their product pages.

The playing field is not fair on Amazon; however, no other platform is fair either. The absence of a single organization's products doesn't concern Amazon. They likely have all the competition for that organization on the platform already. The alternatives of creating a separate e-commerce experience loses the massive audience that Amazon maintains with Prime membership loyalty. As a result, competitive retailers likely don't have the marketing tools to promote products on and off their websites. Amazon has both the audience's attention, the data on their users' activities, and the tools for marketers to take advantage of it all. The goal for Amazon is to offer everything to everyone, with data they are accomplishing. Only organizations that use this information to create relevant advertisements have the opportunity to be a part of the platform's growth.

CHAPTER SIX

Targeting the Consumer's Journey

After attending and speaking at well over a dozen conferences in higher education marketing, a key observation I've made over the years is that marketing is an afterthought for most universities. Excluding for-profit education, the majority of private and public universities appear to view marketing as something they should add only when enrollment is down, funding is tight, or every other university in the state has a marketing department. And so, maybe they should too. The conference attendees I've met from across the United States and the world are perhaps the hardest working professionals in any industry or sector. Yet, to listen to their backgrounds it was rare to hear anyone whose career was solely in higher education marketing. At one Chief Marketing Officer Roundtable, I vividly recall one speaker that spent 20+ years in restaurant marketing. But now, they were at the largest public state university in the country. Another was a member of the English faculty at his small liberal arts college before being selected by the search committee. Still, another spent the last fifteen years running her own public relations agency. She'd only been on her campus six months before appearing on the panel to give career advice in higher education marketing. For most of them, myself included, we all started from somewhere else before coming to higher education. Despite this, we each brought our own views of how marketing should work.

During the seminars at these conferences, I would always try to figure out who was "winning" in the field and why. Did they have more resources and staff? Was it because they had transformational leadership and buy-in from faculty stakeholders? Was their technology stack functional, implemented across the entire school and harmonized together with their entire marketing funnel? I wasn't above copying their techniques if it could work on my campus. I would analyze each part of their campaigns or achievements for something I could replicate. If I could get a copy of their presentations, I would break them apart and look for a speck of gold dust that could change everything for my campaigns. After years of shifting through presentation slides from these conferences, I realized that there was "no one thing" that everyone was doing right. No silver bullet I could find that, if copied, it would make all the difference.

The one mistake I would see again and again was viewing higher education as unique and without comparison. That the process of marketing to students, no matter the demographic, wasn't something that related to other industries or sectors. The higher education recruitment funnel, for instance, was rigid and considered unchangeable by certain offices with responsibilities for student interactions. At the top of the funnel was a suspect level, where the Admissions Office would buy a bulk mailing list of students from the ACT, the SAT, or the College Board. The list would always follow the same criteria of test scores or GPA, within the same states that define their territories, and any other characteristics that matched between the student and the campus from Admission's point of view. The next level was prospects. The student that would express interest and request information directly from the school, providing contact info in exchange. Again, it was the Admissions Office's role to respond to all inquiries. Marketers familiar with the traditional sales funnel will notice the levels flipped between suspect and prospect, where former would usually represent warm leads and the latter cold leads. If the student was interested in the campus, they might proceed to the next level and apply to the school. This level was within the Admission's Office and included multiple stages of the application process that, if completed, would result in an admission decision of either admit or deny. The admitted student would also be told what scholarship funds would be made available to them, if any, should they decide to select the school and make the first deposit. The next level was a handoff of the now matriculated student to the Advising Office for course enrollment. Here, depending on the university, course enrollment could be handled by either the central Advising Office or decentralized offices within underlying colleges or schools of the university. Students would have to call for an appointment weeks in advance. After the enrolled student leaves the recruitment funnel, he or she graduates in four to six years. Hopefully, he or she becomes an active alumnus and future donor.

What was the role of marketing in this funnel? When I arrived in higher education, it was to simply make high-quality brochures and websites for the Admission's Office. Then, get out of the way. When Customer Relationship Management (CRM) platforms entered the landscape because universities could never consider a student, the customer part was relabeled constituent or enrollment. The next marketing role was to make just nice-looking HTML email blasts for when the test boards included an email address or the student inquired. This often left marketing with little more than content and design work. At first, no one outside of marketing cared about response rates, email open percentages, or website conversion rates. The view, even from public state schools, was that higher education was a privilege. Students should not only want to come here but have to overcome administrative barriers and process fatigue to gain entrance. The reality was that students had options. According to the National Association for College Admission Counseling, eighty-two percent of first-time freshmen applied to three or more colleges, while thirty-six percent applied to seven or more colleges in 2015. Both had increased by twenty percent since 1995.[1] Higher education had to adapt to thrive in these new competitive landscapes, and as a result marketing's role, expanded beyond content to include data.

With data, we were able to measure the impact of targeted advertising on suspects that, with raised brand awareness, improved the chances that direct mail pieces didn't get tossed into the recycling bin. Database marketing tactics were applied when buying from test score providers, which created measurable segments and test campaigns in new markets. Direct mail creative was optimized, delivering different messages to each segment tested against control groups in order to validate. Now when potential prospects visited the website for the first time, digital retargeting would follow them until they converted. Likewise, different requests for information webform lengths were tested for completion rates. Within the application process, date timestamps for starting and ending an application were averaged to determine the speed in which a student was moving through the funnel. If the student was moving slower than the average, they were sent a message to encourage completion. Decision days no longer had to just be the Admissions Office telethons. Testimonial campaigns would be live weeks before generating positive brand experiences. The hand-off to advising and the difficulties of getting appointments were overcome with online scheduling services, that reminded students of appointments on their smartphone calendars and nudged those who hadn't booked an appointment yet. The more I looked at marketing along the journey, it was clear that no one path was ever the same. In truth, it was always a combination of strategies and tactics, the courage to fail, and the necessity of trial and error that proved the value of data.

Choose Your Own Adventure

The most common approach to looking at the consumer's journey is to use the marketing funnel developed by American advertising and sales pioneer E. St. Elmo Lewis in 1898.[2] It depicts a linear view of the journey using the funnel analogy to represent the dwindling mass audiences moving from each stage to the next. It starts with the awareness stage, which at this point, could be both of a particular brand or of overall products and services in a category. Next is the interest stage, where it is common to assume they are seeking more information specific to the product or service, its price, places where it is available, and any additional promotional material that is part of the standard marketing mix. The consumer then reaches the decision stage on whether to purchase the product or service, which while following the interest stage, has no specified timetable for when they might reach this stage. Directly following and the last stage of the funnel is the action

Figure 6.1. Illustration by team Charcoal of AIDA funnel.
Lewis, E. St. Elmo. Financial Advertising. New York : Garland Pub, 1985.
https://trove.nla.gov.au/version/22406169.

stage of purchasing that product or service (fig. 6.1). The Lewis funnel is also referred to as the AIDA, purchase, or sales funnel. It has perhaps the largest amount of literature supporting it and variations building upon or within it. The simplicity of the funnel explains a lot about its longevity and reach outside of marketing into the organizational c-suites of leadership. A weakness of the funnel is a lack of post or repeat purchase elements that account for brand loyalty. This can likely be explained by the era of its creation predating the concept of national or global brand marketing.

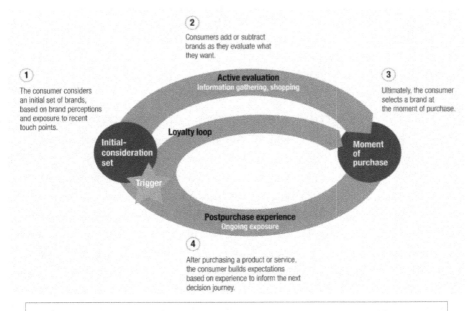

Figure 6.2. Court, David, Dave Elzinga, Susan Mulder, and Ole Jørgen Vetvik. "The Consumer Decision Journey | McKinsey." McKinsey Quarterly, June 2009. https://www.mckinsey.com/business-functions/ marketing-and-sales/our-insights/the-consumer-decision-journey.

The next innovation in understanding consumer journey was more than a hundred years later in 2009 from the global consulting firm McKinsey. Researchers looked at the purchase decisions of almost 20,000 consumers across five industries and three continents.[3] Instead of a funnel, they formulated a loop that started at the brand consideration phase where an initial set of brands are considered regarding a product or service. The consumer then moves to the active evaluation phase where the brand set may expand as the consumer seeks more information and starts the shopping process. Ultimately the consumer reaches the moment of purchase, selecting one brand for the product or service. Instead of ending, the consumer now reaches the post-purchase experience phase where the ongoing exposure to the purchase determines whether it was a positive or negative experience. This triggers whether the loop is repeated with the same brand as the consumer enters the loyalty loop phase. Or a new brand consideration phase is created with the previously purchased brand removed (fig. 6.2). In practice, this model hinges on touchpoints with the brand both before and after purchase. Meanwhile, more emphasis is placed on providing information at key moments in the loop when the customer is seeking to reward loyalty behavior. The simplicity of the loop, however, undermines the complexity of the decision journey for consumers.

Modern Consumer Decision-Making Journey

Until recently, no model existed that provided a comprehensive view of the consumer journey and detailed touchpoints where marketing might encourage that journey. Enter the *Modern Consumer Decision-Making Journey* by Mark Michael at Deloitte, created in 2018. It has made the rounds at marketing conferences like Digital Summit, Internet Summit, and American Marketing Association.[4] It improves upon previous models by considering the consumer consideration sets flowing in both a positive and negative direction. It expands the number of stages more than doubling previous models. It also accounts for brand loyalty, both as an active consideration for which is advocated and a passive consideration to which is subscribed. This new subscription journey can be seen in platforms like Amazon's Prime membership, music entertainment services like Pandora, Spotify, or Apple Music, and monthly delivery box companies like Blue Apron and Dollar Shave Club. It is also the only model to consider which stages include engagement opportunities by the brand to influence the consumer. This model serves as the backdrop for the consumer journey in the rest of this chapter. Each stage will look at the intent of the consumer as it relates to a brand's product or service, while considering which data points might be available and from what source. Then, for the marketers, it will inform which channels, tactics, and messages are needed to guide the consumer forward. Finally, it will guide you toward where conversion points might be placed to determine success (fig. 6.3).

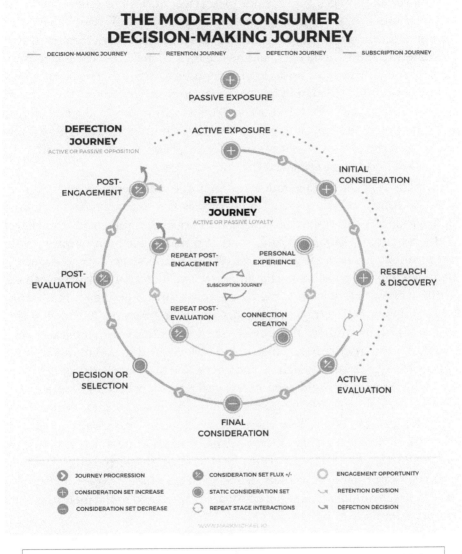

Figure 6.3. Michael, Mark. "The Modern Consumer Decision-Making Journey." Mark Michael. Accessed December 6, 2019. https://www.markmichael.io/insights/the-modern-consumer-customer-decision-making-journey.

The journey begins with the passive exposure stage, where the customers are not yet shopping for a product or service. Still, he or she is exposed to messaging from marketing, media, and content. At this stage, the consumer does not yet have any intent. Market research to determine target consumers brand awareness should be the measurement at this stage. Mass marketing channels like radio, television, online video, programmatic audio, and display advertising could be used to raise that awareness. Messages at this stage should be more about brand benefits within the product or service category. Brand perception from market research can help determine if the brand has reached the consumer's top of mind, as with increased familiarity of the likelihood of entering the consideration set.

The active exposure stage follows as an initial consideration set forms for brands around a certain product or service as the consumers seek relevant information. At this stage, the consumer is now intent on an action related to the product or service. Again, market research for brand awareness is best positioned to provide data points related to this stage, while measuring the percentage of consumers that are now considering making a purchase in this category are within a fixed amount of time. The digital marketing tactic of impression, retargeting, occurs when the consumer has to view the creative. It is added during the previous stage for online video, programmatic audio, and display channels. Then, it can be leveraged to add more targeted messages to previously reached audiences. With impression retargeting, marketing messages could then be layered and sequential. These ensures the intent to nurture the consumer along the initial stages, while time-delayed messages could be separated by different campaign weeks to showcase different benefits. Moreover, promotional offers not available in the previous stage could exist at this level to entice preferred consideration. Marketers can then look at their increases in the share of voice within the market, determining the amount of organic search and social mentions that occur compared to competitors.

Organizations with a high degree of brand awareness are most likely to enter the initial consideration stage. During this stage, the consumer is now active with both the product or service category and the inclusion of the relevant brands. Some brands may enter this stage because of the proximity to the consumer in either physical location or availability of meeting the consumers desired criteria. Website traffic analytics is one of the best sources of data points at this stage, as it is likely a consumer will visit the first time with an intent of learning more or making a purchase. Geolocation tracking can also be useful at this stage, for it monitors if the consumer is or has visited a physical retail location. Therefore, both website and geolocation retargeting are ideal marketing tactics to remain in the consideration set as well, since marketing messages aimed at furthering the journey move customers to the next stage. Points of conversions to consider for the website are time spent on the website, the number of pages visited, and return traffic from retargeting campaigns. Marketers looking at physical locations and geolocation should consider conversion points like return store visits, and online visitation again from the retargeting campaigns.

Consumers now enter the research and discovery stage, where they seek to inform themselves about the brands within their considerations set. Consumers will use whatever methods are at their disposal like search and social at this stage; however, they are not limited by any platform. In truth, this stage can occur simply in the store as he or she looks at shelves of products, or just as easily as an Amazon or Google search result page. This stage perhaps has the most amount of data points to consider like organic search keywords, product or service reviews, and even requests for information forms. All can double as conversion points. It doesn't get any easier for marketers when considering channels and tactics either, as the full range of demand generation tactics are viable at this stage across search, social, and programmatic channels. The noise to signal ratio at this stage can be troubling, however, the doubling down on attribution model building from chapter two can help reduce or solves this issue. Measurements that can be labeled consumer outreach offers the best data points for conversion tracking and behavior.

Once the consumer has the information they've deemed as important in their journey, they have reached the active evaluation stage. Here the consumer intends to review their consideration set to begin the process of subtracting brands before moving to the next stage. The consumer can also decide to add the consideration set, requiring that they returned and the journey back to the research and discovery stage to review the addition. Websites that offer comparative selection tools will often have crucial data points from this stage. Activity from the consumer will also appear to increase as the possible frequency of return traffic. Outreach engagement with sales or customer service personnel, or even concurrent web sessions from a single device, allow customers to browse across multiple open web browser tabs while reviewing products. For brands that had not previously entered the consideration set, this is an important stage to make their most powerful argument. The final pitch is also important for brands in the consideration set. After all, the passive exposure stage isn't the time to lose the consumer. While all marketing channels should still be considered, the more competitive tactics are critical to success at this stage. It is not enough to simply promote the brand benefits but to also go aggressively on the offensive. By doing this, you enter the consideration set or defensive and remain in the consideration set. The only losing strategy is to pretend the brand's superiority is beyond reproach. Conversion points at this stage can be the activity or engagement that shows the consumer reached this stage. But ultimately, it is found at the conclusion of the next stage.

For some brands, the journey to the final consideration stage is where the consideration set narrows down to a few remaining brands. In retrospect, it is a hard-fought process. Others may find themselves at this stage all the time based on the strength of their brand awareness, product or service attributes, or compelling marketing mix. The intent of the consumer here is clear. Make a final selection and choose the one brand above all else. Few data sources exist outside the conversion at this stage. For e-commerce products, an online shopping cart is one possible data point. This leaves marketing tactics at this stage to focus on shopping cart abandonment tactics via retargeting tactics. Meanwhile, services and products purchased outside an online presence should continue to rely on retargeting methods. This is the last stage for which marketing messages should include a promotional offer to avoid confusion after the purchase. The only real conversion point here is either the decision stage or the selection stage that follows it, thereby completing the transaction by the consumer. This stage has no engagement opportunity for brands.

After the initial purchase, the consumer then moves to the post-evaluation stage where they begin to experience the selected brand's product or service. While the intent is still a factor of experience, consumers are generally in a reaction phase. He or she is still determining if the brand promise has been delivered. Customer satisfaction research, or net promoter surveys, can help provide insight at this level on whether this experience has been positive or negative for the consumer. Ideally, way before this stage, customer contact info like telephone numbers and emails were collected. These were acquired with permission to contact them to follow up on the purchase. This makes email a scalable form of engagement and channel for outreach, where messages can now be about getting the most value from the product or service. Email open percentages and survey response rates are ideal conversion points at this stage because they provide the data points to measure the experience level.

The final stage of the decision-making journey is the post-engagement stage where the consumer might share their experience from the prior stage with other consumers using word of mouth, social media, or writing product reviews. Data sources for this match the engagement. Social media monitoring and reviews will catch those data points. Meanwhile, brand awareness research can look to measure the impact of word of mouth. The same channel that worked in the prior stage, email, is back again where customers that provided positive feedback via surveys in the previous channel should immediately be asked to provide reviews of the product and share on social media. Depending on the platform or website where the purchase occurred, marketing messages offering a discount on future purchases can be sent for successful completion, unless it's prevented by platform rules like Amazon. The successful completion of a review or social media share then acts as the conversion point of this stage. A negative experience, however, can lead to a defection journey that can move consumers back to any previous stage looking for alternatives or substitutions for the brand's product or service.

Retention Journey

A common business adage is that retaining a customer is cheaper than acquiring a new customer. With the modern consumer decision-making journey model, that assumption is given validation. The retention journey illustrates (fig. 6.4) far fewer stages for the inner loop compared with the overall journey model. The Lewis AIDA funnel lacks this entire process, assuming a consumer would have to repeat the full funnel. The McKinley model shows only a single Loyalty Loop phase, while Mr. Michael's model accounts for four stages that center on customer experience. So while it might be cheaper to retain customers, it doesn't get any easier in terms of effort by the brand.

The personal experience stage kicks off the retention journey as consumers builds their perception of the brand's product or service based on of course their experience. The intent here is pure emotional reaction. Does the product or service add value to their life? Is it solving problems? Was it worth it to begin with? While email would remain a strong tactic at this stage, another channel to consider is adding a time-delayed

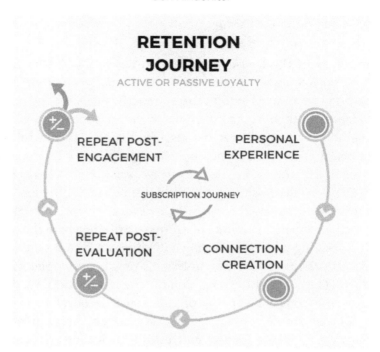

Figure 6.4. Michael, Mark. "Retention Journey from The Modern Consumer Decision-Making Journey." Mark Michael. Accessed December 6, 2019. https://www.markmichael.io/insights/the-modern-consumer-customer-decision-making-journey.

retargeting layer to the decision or selection stage. This would allow the appearance of marketing messages to arrive after the purchase but before additional purchases in the journey. The important marketing message to convey here is to reinforce the choice as positive in order to set up engagement opportunities in follow-up stages. The simplest measurement of conversions within this loop is retaining the consumer for additional purchases, leaving more nuanced data-points to look at in regard to the customer satisfaction scores.

The next stage, connection creation, is a make-or-break moment for a brand within the retention journey. Now, not only does the previous product or service have to produce a positive experience, but so do the subsequent brand offerings. The history of business is littered with examples of missteps in this area from New Coke, Microsoft Zune, Google+, and many more.

The difficulty in repeatedly producing and maintaining an "aha moment" each time the consumer rounds the retention journey is perhaps the most difficult stage of the entire model. Success at this stage can also come in many forms, like the first-time loyalty reward. Points are redeemed from a credit card or membership program. The rush that comes with hitting the jackpot at the casino or winning the level of a video game keeps the player engaged for longer. A sports franchise's longtime fans are awarded not just by the occasional win, but rather a championship victory. For example, St. Louis fans were awarded with the Blues Stanley Cup championship after fifty-two years in 2019, or the measurable signs of weight loss from diet programs like Jenny Craig or Weight Watchers. When once separate or difficult technical products become wonderfully simplified, it creates an interconnected experience in the case of Apple products. Whatever the product or service category, understanding the connection creation stage is both an engagement opportunity and a data-point that should be collected. The marketing channel might best be pulled back from targeted efforts to widely broadcast awareness at this stage. Both those inside and outside of the retention journey convey the full emotional impact of this moment to all consumers. To perhaps be bold at this moment by reworking philosopher and media theorist Marshall McLuhan[5], the moment is the message. Realistically, the experience that the consumer has is more important than the marketing message or channels that can convey it. To put it another way, all the marketing in the world cannot overcome the lack of experience by the consumer. Without it, there is no journey to continue.

The last two stages of the retention journey are repeats of the post-evaluation and post-engagement stages, respectfully. The only difference now is that the consumer has more points of experience with the brand then their initial purchase. Similar engagement opportunities and data-points exist here, just as they did previously. What's new, however, is the ability to compare data-points from previous and initial journeys in order to measure if the experience is improving or reaching a breaking point for the consumer where they might exit the journey.

The strongest argument for the use of *The Modern Consumer Decision-Making Journey* over prior attempts to map this process is the inclusion of the subscription journey. Nestled within the retention journey is the distinction that the consumer is no longer in an active intent mindset but rather a passive repeating purchase cycle. It is frictionless and perhaps automated. Mr. Michael makes the point that the concept of subscriptions isn't a new business model when considering milk being delivered to doorsteps and having newspapers tossed into a consumer's yard by a delivery person. A distinction should be made between true subscription models and product or services on contract payments like with cellular carriers or in the case of certain utility services. This includes cable television or home internet, where an alternative provider may not be available in some areas. That still leaves plenty of popular subscriptions to consider like video-stream entertainment services in the form of Netflix, Hulu, and HBO Now, as well as monthly box subscriptions like Bird Box, Stitch Fix, and Loot Crate. Everything from wine to cheese, socks to handbags, book clubs and kids craft projects has exploded to every imaginable category within the subscription e-commerce market. The subscription e-commerce market has grown by more than 100 percent a year over the past five years. The largest such retailers generated more than $2.6 billion in sales in 2016, up from a mere $57.0 million in 2011.[6] A defining characteristic across all subscriptions is the convenience for the consumer. Why check local or cable listings for anything interesting that might be playing, when thousands of shows are available to watch on demand? Why hassle with figuring out recipes and ingredients to make for dinner when it can be delivered to the door fresh and ready to be cooked? Need something to wear in a certain size, while fashionably couture? Now, entire selections can be sent without the expense of a personal shopper.

While business implications to an organization of an automated repeating purchase cycle subscription fee is undeniably tempting, the challenge is more than just having a recurring payment option and products to ship or services to provide. The subscription journey might also be the most difficult journey to achieve for brands since they have to continuously provide value to the consumer in order to keep them in a passive mode. Marketers must also be consistently moving new consumers through the initial *Modern Consumer Decision-Making Journey*. Likewise, they must retain subscribers with similar tactics from the retention journey as well.

Data Abhors a Vacuum

In order to appreciate *The Modern Consumer Decision-Making Journey*, marketers have to embrace its complexity. Perhaps this is why the AIDA model has persisted for over a hundred years. It is simple to understand and explain to leadership. However, forcing the fit of the intricacies of available data within simple models is an unworkable and futile effort. The challenge of a functioning data democracy necessitates a usable paradigm for the data that forms around the consumer journey.

The abundance of data available from within the consumer journey now is neither limited to large organizations nor sophisticated platforms. Market research methods and customer satisfaction surveys can monitor before and after the decision or selection behavior. All the while, digital marketing reports and website analytics can provide feedback in many stages as well. The consumer can also provide data for more points of reference. Therefore, the consumers don't just trip and fall into filling out a request for information form. Still, just having the data isn't enough. It must be applied by marketing in order to improve the consumer journey.

Marketers should also look for what data is missing when looking at the consumer journey. Are there false assumptions about how the data should be used because of the "that's the way we've always done it" mentality? Identify which data points are the pain points for the consumer by not only the feedback they are sending but also by the actions they are not taking in the journey. Develop a plan on how to use the available data. This not only validates the decision or selection stage but also tests for improvements. Stuart Hogg, Director of Strategic Development and Operations at McCann Worldgroup, has worked with a number of Fortune 500 brands. He advises marketers to make sure to create hypotheses around why new communication touchpoints will improve the customer journey. Then, implement and test them. If the hypotheses are wrong, go back to the journey's map, to reassess, to tweak, and to improve.[7] In short, always be testing.

Because business goals are built on outcomes, marketing goals typically follow suit. However, focusing on the destination instead of the journey won't create any new opportunities along the way. Analyzing the available data, looking for missing data points, and seeking pattern recognition from available sources, can all reveal possible new tactics, channels, or even audiences unknown to the business. It doesn't have to end at improving marketing strategies. Data from the consumer journey can improve website user experiences, customer services, product or services development. Data stops being just intelligence. Instead, it becomes the voice and vote of the consumer on whether a product wins or loses.

CHAPTER SEVEN

Personalization at Scale

By its peak in 2004, Blockbuster had 60,000 employees and 9,000 stores worldwide with revenues of $5.9 billion.[1] Before most households had access to broadband internet, few legitimate online videos platforms existed. So for most consumers, that meant DVD or VHS as a home entertainment alternative to broadcast television. While limited by physical space, every Blockbuster still offered over a hundred options with new releases cycling in each month.

The summer before I joined the military was also the year Blockbuster offered a tier rewards program for their members nationwide. A Blockbuster rental membership was free, and the rewards program was $9.95 a year.[2] After so many rentals in a year, you could reach gold status that included unlimited rentals and a free classic movie with each rental. Because I loved watching movies, not just new releases, I racked up a lot of free rentals — well, over a hundred that summer. This also meant I likely paid to rent close to 200 videos in total that year.

Enjoying all those movies like I did had one major drawback. As time progressed, it got harder to find movies I hadn't seen and harder still to figure out which movies I might enjoy in the store. Even though the rental might have been free, I didn't want to lose the opportunity cost on a bad movie. I'm sure I would spend close to an hour on some days trying to find a movie. Almost none of the employees were helpful either. Many had spent less time with movies than I did, and most would just point me towards the more expensive new releases.

Blockbuster had plenty of data points to assist with my movie search. It had all the data on every single movie I watched and could make suggestions on movie habits similar to other Blockbuster members. They had how often I visited the store as well as the length of my average rental. This would have given them the time between visits to make suggestions on future rentals. As a member, they had both my mailing address and an email address to deliver suggestions and find the optimal channel for delivery that created a response. Finally, their point of sale system could process coupons that could be used to track conversions and monitor which movie titles they suggested were correct to my tastes. All this was possible that summer. From a technology point of view, instead all I remember were generic buy-one-get-one coupon offers for free rentals that I used. I additionally had discounts on movie snacks that my purchase history would have shown zero redemptions. Still, as long as I continued to rent movies, why would Blockbuster have to innovate or personalize my experience?

In the years that followed however, Blockbuster's business model was under attack on several fronts. Their main product supply of new movie rentals had traditionally featured a blackout period where new releases were only available for rent before they went on sale several weeks later. However, major movie studios like Warner Bros. eliminated this period in favor of direct sales making exclusive deals with retail stores like Wal-Mart. By doing this, it allowed them to bypass Blockbuster in-movie sales for the distributors.[3] Then along came new competitors like Redbox that offered a movie rental via a vending machine set-up. It eliminated the need for membership cards of traditional video rental companies, stocking only a few in-demand new releases, and creating a convenience factor by co-locating with higher traffic fast-food restaurants and twenty-four-hour pharmacy retail chains. Then came the proverbial David to Blockbuster's Goliath, Netflix. Decades before they became the online video streaming giant, Netflix innovated where the Blockbuster Video store model failed. Membership wasn't a plastic laminated card to keep next to a library card, but rather an online account that was part of the service making them more like users than customers. Netflix users could rent an unlimited amount of movies each month, keeping them as long as they like. Members both received and returned movies, but not to any physical location. Instead, they used the U.S. Postal Service back to a distribution warehouse. Then the next movie in the user's queue would arrive in a few days. When the queue moved from the physical DVDs to streaming video, data mattered to Netflix. The strength of their model relied on users continuously seeing value from their subscription by having more movies staged in their queue. This method required a robust recommendation algorithm for the service. Netflix would go so far as to crowdsource and award a million-dollar cash prize to anybody that could improve their recommendation code by just ten percent. The data set to work with included over 100 million ratings of 17,770 movies from 480,189 users.[4] There is more to the story of Blockbuster's downfall, however, maintaining loyalty with customers versus alternatives was a major factor. It would have required personalization at a scale of more than just one rewards member at a single store over the summer. This means more than just the availability of data. It is how those data points are connected to provide value, because the alternative of avoiding personalization is to risk becoming the last Blockbuster store in America.[5]

Greeting Card Content

Platforms have mastered the concept of personalization at scale, while marketing has only scratched the surface. For platforms, personalization is a feature. The result of algorithms have supplied massive amounts of data by users. Yet marketers for decades have treated personalization like a greeting card, where if they just put the customers first name above a templated message meant for anyone, that made it personalized. This isn't the result of a lack of data but rather the underutilization of marketing tools in favor of generic content.

This type of content can be seen in communication plans that are one dimensional, lacking both depth and consideration of the available data points. The marketing campaign has only one story to tell, across all mediums, at all times. Returning to the axiom of the right audience with the right message at the right time, this singular strategy has but one chance to succeed with just generic content. And yet, if that had any chance of success, marketers wouldn't worry about ad frequency or digital retargeting channels.

This is not to argue that marketers shouldn't tell the brand story for their product or service. Nor that all content regardless of medium is doomed to fail. Every marketer can likely point to at least one piece of content in a campaign and produce evidence of its success in achieving results. But rather, it concerns the approach of producing content without regard for data only to then include some personalization during the distribution as a way to greet the consumer. It does not achieve the scale necessary in a data democracy.

The way to achieve personalization at scale is to incorporate dynamic content in marketing messages. Dynamic content is when different data points are used to determine which content elements display for the consumer in a single message.[6] This customization is made possible by marketing automation platforms, which improves upon previous methods to achieve this outcome. Though, doing this is required in order to separate messages to each segmented audience. The desired result is messages that appear smart and immersive to the consumer. Smart, because it takes into account the data which is available. It meets the consumer where they are in their journey. Immersive, because the content is consistent with their intent, based on the collection of data points with the attributes of the product or service, in which the consumer is interested.

HELLO: My Name Is

Content can only improve with the inclusion of data in all parts of the process. There are several ways to consider data points when creating content and incorporating that data into the message. The method requires not just data for personalization but also marketing automation platforms. Both can merge or create content from it. Before considering any new marketing tools, a strategy behind personalization is needed. It uses techniques like association, visitation, connection, recommendation, and location.

Personalization by association is finding like data points between those that have purchased a product or service and those that are interested. These similarities should be enough to form sizable audiences but not so few that it only produces a few large segments. Also, not so many that only a handful of people are in each audience and there are more segments than stars in the sky. Like ancient mariners using constellations for navigation, marketers should use these data points to test strategies to find their way amongst these segments. Then, test and determine which strategies produce repeatable results. This technique has the loosest criteria to form segments, therefore perhaps it is the widest possible application. A robust example of consumer segmentation along associations would be Experian's

Mosaic household-based consumer lifestyle segmentation. It classifies over 126 million households in the United States along seventy-one unique segments within nineteen groups. These associations are built using socio-demographics, lifestyles, behaviors, and culture data points that Experian collects. Likewise, they are all consumers in its function as a credit bureau.[7] Even better than just being an example, marketers can also connect their data to Experian to discover which Mosaic segments their consumers are in. Then, customize both message content and marketing channels to better reach then convert those audiences.

To create personalization by visitation, consumers, of course, need something to visit. However, to allow for data, the visits must be trackable. Each must produce different variable results. More importantly, the place visited must be able to dynamically alter its experience based on data variables. The most common place where this is possible are websites. Here, data points like pages visited, content is viewed, it tracks how often a user visited. The source of traffic can all be used to create audience segments. Dynamic content can then be served on the website for these segments, testing against control groups with no modifications, to determine which perform better in producing action. A well-publicized example of this technique also happens to provide personalization technology for websites. Optimizely, it created twenty-six different versions of the homepage. Each was uniquely customized for a different segment. These homepage experiences were created for named accounts that were current or prospective customers of Optimizely, and also by industry visitors like travel. Therefore, they could make a strong use case, by geography for North America, Europe, or Asia-Pacific visitors or customers who had an Optimizely login cookie on their browser.[8]

The mass adoption and utilization of social media platforms make personalization by connections of the customer's social network achievable. These connections are now available data points instead of inaccessible address books and family trees. These connectors do not have to be to direct, since friends of friends or indirect associates with high clout could be used to show social proof for the product or service. While some social media platforms have advertising options and social plugins that can show how many friends "like" a brand, content personalization for connection requires data points between both who likes it and what they like about it. These data points can be collected in many different ways, much like personalized quizzes. Buzzfeed pioneered this form of personalization on social media. It created personality quizzes that, on average, were shared up to 1,900 times. These quizzes are similar to healthcare risk assessments, financial calculators, and other business-to-business data collection methods. This is how energy supplier and producer Eneco created a personalized quiz that, in just six weeks, generated over 1,000 emails from potential clients providing relevant information in return for that which they'd been looking.[9]

While other strategies for personalization are focused on influencing the next consumer, a recommendation technique leverages data from the last consumer who purchased the product or service. Instead of hoping that post-purchase delight will lead to word of mouth style referral, the content could be created for them to share with their colleagues, friends, and family. This is based on the attributes they found most satisfying about the product or service. A multitude of services exists for marketers to leverage this technique. These focus on requesting online reviews, building brand ambassadors, and referral programs. More importantly, a strategy is needed to take advantage of results, for example, by creating a reward for each recommendation. Online storage company Dropbox increased signups by sixty percent. Uber ride-sharing service gave users referral codes to invite friends, each gaining credits for free rides. The more friends that joined, the more credit could be earned. Airbnb online marketplace, known for arranging or offering lodging, designed an incentive program where both recipient and referrer were eligible if the recipient booked a place to stay. Yet, they went further. They tripled the reward if the recipient also made their place available for booking. Thus, it created both supply and demand from their customers.[10]

Personalization by location uses data associated with either the previous, present, or possible future location of a consumer. This data is available from device history, IP addresses information, and purchase history when considering physical locations. Customer accounts that require a zip code to create and also zip code data from credit card purchases can also be used to determine where they are from. In most cases. dynamic content can then be localized to marketing messages for that area. This is perhaps the most common technique used by large organizations today, along with a national or global presence. It may also be the oldest technique for circulation of coupon offers by mailing zip codes. Beyond that simplicity, brands like Home Depot geofenced all their stores to offer localized design trends and products with their mobile application, acting as an in-store guide. The NBA Sacramento Kings use location to improve fan experience, showing open parking sports, closest bars, and ordering food delivery to the fan's seat.[11]

Just Scale It

If traditional content marketers approached personalization without dynamic content, they would only see the need for more content for each audience segment. This approach doesn't scale when considering all the ways that personalization is possible with available data points, because each audience segment would need its piece of static content. Dynamic content allows marketers to skip excessive content and use the right marketing platforms. Thus, it builds adaptable marketing messages to reflect different audience segments.

While there are hundreds of different marketing platforms available to marketers from many companies, a specific combination is required to achieve dynamic content. First, a centralized marketing database stores customer data and interaction history with the organization's product or service. This will likely not be the only marketing database but should act as the central unified database to assemble all the data points for each audience. Next, a smart content generator that is informed by the database either shows or hides content based on the rules set by the marketer. Then, there is a website with dynamic web pages that is easily editable and typically marketing-controlled, rather than run through another department like IT. It is connected to the database via an application programming interface (API) bridge. Finally, an integrated email system extends dynamic content to email marketing messages that is tied to the database.[12]

Once the platforms, databases, and websites are connected, building the marketing messages with dynamic content can begin. To begin, consider which audience segments for personalization are relevant to the marketing messages for the customer journey. Review what data points are needed for these segments. Check to see if any large groups of customers in the database have insufficient data to be part of these new segments. Develop a process to request these missing data points from the groups, while ensuring that a process exists to collect all needed data points from future customers. Each marketing message's design needs to include dynamic content and how that content will be different for each audience segment. Include trackable objects and outcomes into each dynamic content area, so that results can be measured against each audience segment. Then, be sure to test each marketing message for each possible audience segment. This includes dynamic content variation for coherency. Once a series of marketing messages are deployed using dynamic content, marketers should continue testing for improvements. Do this for audience segments, which is to expand personalization variations, and conversion optimization. With more data points comes the possibility for dynamic content to expand. More products or services, customers, and their interactions make for possible audience segments over time.

Moneyball Fandom

Few companies represent the era of data democracy and the usage of dynamic content as well as e-commerce sports merchandise retailer Fanatics. While likely not recognizable as a brand for the majority of consumers, their technology drives the merchandise websites for the NFL, MLB, MLS, NBA, NHL, and Nascar, as well as more than 200 college and professional sports teams.[13] More than just a company that is good at making licensing deals with sports leagues, Fanatics features all the hallmarks of an organization that has mastered elements of personalization by using connected marketing platforms to reach a sports fan in moments of peak fandom.

In 2016, Fanatics generated over 27,000 personalized marketing campaigns by sending 3.8 billion email messages. One campaign personalization example was when professional football player Peyton Manning announced his retirement on March 2016. Fanatics was able to send custom emails targeted to fans who had expressed interest in Manning in the past, including the Denver Broncos fans, Indianapolis Colts fans, and people in Tennessee, where Manning went to college. In an interview that year, Matt Smith, VP of CRM at Fanatics remarked that, "We've known for a while that our business is in large part driven by really special moments, whether it's a particular play or a player crossing a milestone or a team winning a championship. The same things that we see on TV or at a game that drives excitement also drives interest in our product and our industry. Our ability to capitalize on those moments when fans are feeling some of their deepest feelings towards their own teams is really important to us."[14] By looking for data points that connected Manning retiring with those who were interested in him in the past, the teams he played on, and the fans of his alma mater, Fanatics combined personalization of both association and location.

To capture moments of peak fandom, Fanatics built a unified marketing platform. It scales based on where the fans are as users when moments occur that start their consumer journey. Then, it removes barriers that prevent conversions. Matt Madrigal, Fanatics' chief technical officer, participated in an interview with Quartz that the focused on being a "mobile-first" company. Almost eighty percent of their customers use mobile, with the intent on "building once, leveraging everywhere." This allowed Fanatics' to be everywhere. The potential consumer is including at the game, at the bar, or watching sports at home because this is everywhere the user would have their smartphone. By making it easier to buy on mobile, the more likely to have a conversion, which is why over half of Fanatics' sales are made on mobile devices and during live moments. By having a dynamic website that is part of their marketing platforms and not a separate experience, they can also leverage consumer location in their personalization. The website is connected to a centralized marketing database Fanatic calls "Cloud Commerce." According to Madrigal, it tracks every click, search, and purchase on every site run by Fanatics. It further tracks emails, ads, and sales from physical stores. The Cloud Commerce platform also monitors social media and the news for information on players like injuries or trades. Then, it automatically surfaces and re-ranks products, and flags unusual events, like a spike in searches for a minor or unknown player. This approach is key to their unique selling proposition amongst sports fandom by allowing for more flexibility to generate smart content when interest peaks in a player at any time. For example, a traditional sports retail chain like Modell's or Dick's might have to choose which jerseys to stock for each team before the season starts. So, after player drafts, they'll only ask for jerseys of the most well-known players from the draft. Fanatics team members, however, can use Photoshop to quickly create jersey mock-ups for the site. The system promotes them to relevant customers and those who have shown interest in the team before. So when a Dallas Cowboys' backup linebacker, Leighton Vander Esch, was given a chance to play, recording thirteen tackles and an interception, following only his fourth professional appearance, he was named the NFL's defensive player of the week. Fanatics saw a spike in interest, so they quickly ensured his jersey was ready for any customer who wanted to buy it. Finally, with their integrated email system in the Commerce Cloud, Fanatics can alert fans of a team regarding new products seconds after each pick in the NFL Draft.[15]

The unpredictable nature of sports, where any given game can produce winners and losers, defies the odds. It produces record-breaking moments, or the business side of trades. Likewise, free-agents and retirements can produce thousands of micro-moments in any given season. By combining personalization in each of these moments, with a marketing platform built to scale in response, Fanatics is ready for both the small and big moments in every fan's community. When the Broncos won the Super Bowl in 2016, only their fifteen million fans received messages offering new championship apparel from Fanatics seconds after the win. Panthers fans, on the other hand, didn't receive any notification.[16]

Who's Watching Who?

In perhaps the twilight of Blockbuster's years, lacking a crystal ball to predict the future, it reckoned another axiom of the business world. If you can't beat them, buy them. Or at least try. But that's what happened multiple times throughout the early 2000s. Netflix CEO and co-founder Reed Hastings courted a deal with then-Blockbuster CEO John Antioco to purchase the then DVD-by-mail rental company for $50 million. In 2019, the company now has a market cap of $127 billion.[17] Of course, the devil is in the details. Netflix was still a decade away from streaming technology and was reportedly hemorrhaging money. While pitching that they were merging to take over Blockbuster's unrealized DVD-by-mail service, they left Blockbuster to run the retail stores. Plenty of ink has been spent debating this missed opportunity, while it seems Netflix has never looked back. Instead, they built an advantage in user personalization which was unrivaled in the streaming business.

As *The Modern Consumer Decision Making-Journey* model from chapter six makes clear, it's necessary to maintain the subscription journey. A continuous cycle must delight the consumer and make it easy for them to stay avoiding alternatives. For Netflix, this means providing users with the constant discovery of content that meets their unique needs. To accomplish this, Netflix uses personalization by visitation. They gather data points from the content the user visits and views to build a user profile tailored to their preferences. In an interview, Netflix's vice president of product innovation, Todd Yellin, stated that profiles are built using several kinds of data. These include what people watch, what they watch after, what they watch before, what they watched a year ago. Moreover, it includes what they've watched recently and at what time of day. This behavior data is sorted by sophisticated machine-learning algorithms, which place each viewer into a "taste community" of which there are a couple thousand variations. It adds personalization by association, that affect what recommendations pop up to the top of Netflix's on-screen interface. As a result, genre rows are displayed, and how each row is ordered varies for each user.[18]

Netflix's approach to personalization doesn't end at discovery, but instead takes their massive data trove of user-profiles and data points to develop what is likely the most expensive dynamic content available anywhere. After launching its streaming video on demand platform in 2007, Netflix shifted the focus away from the DVD-by-mail service. Subscribers continued to skyrocket with the addition of original programming. It was an attempt to get ahead of early competitors in the space that was only focused on licensing content from other studios. However, instead of approaching original programming content the traditional way by reviewing television show pilots like a network would or just flexing a large budget and ordering a ton of content while hoping something resonates with users, they approached it with a data-driven creative strategy. In 2011, Netflix reportedly ordered two full seasons of a *House of Cards* remake without seeing a single scene because it was convinced the show would be a big hit. David Fincher was both directing and producing the series and it starred Kevin Spacey. This was possible because of the data points available from users watching Kevin Spacey, movies by David Fincher, and viewership of the original *House of Cards*, which they were licensing from the BBC. Netflix had an edge that others lacked. As their communication director, Jonathan Friedland said in an interview, "We know what people watch on Netflix and, with a high degree of confidence, we're able to understand how big a likely audience is for a given show based on people's viewing habits."[19] The show would go on to be a big hit for Netflix for several seasons, winning both new subscribers and award shows. This strategy for personalized content leverages both association and recommendation approaches since the user acts as both the data point for potential show success and as the advocate to promote its existence to others with similar viewing habits.

While not every brand has the same resources as Netflix does to develop personalization at scale with original content, like Fanatics, both organizations began smaller. They keep a focus on data that translates to recommendations. Instead of developing products or services the same way as every competitor, they leveraged data as an advantage to improve not copy. This shows that content needn't be one size that fits all but can reach the right audience with the right message at the right time with the right data.

CHAPTER EIGHT

Building a Data Democracy

Continuing education and professional programs have been a hallmark of Washington University in St. Louis since 1908. Founded officially in 1931 as the professional and continuing education division of the College of Arts & Sciences within Washington University, University College has been serving the St. Louis region ever since. University College offers more than forty programs of study, with programs at every level. These include associate, certificates, undergraduate degrees, post-baccalaureate certificates, advanced certificates, and graduate degrees helping students advance their careers. All students can explore new fields, while growing personally and professionally. However, by 2016, when I arrived as the director of marketing and communications, University College faced serious issues. Enrollments had been declining by about five percent for several years.

Most of the people living in St. Louis were unaware of the availability of programs at University College. From my viewpoint, I had worked professionally in the St. Louis market the majority of my adult life, while being unaware of University College. I worked specifically in higher education marketing for several years. While aware of Washington University, I was still unaware of the University College division until I applied for the job. I was a part-time student in the evening for both my bachelor's and master's degrees. But still, I was unaware that University College had these types of programs, at least as I studied at another university less than forty miles away. I was a veteran student, so University College offered the Yellow Ribbon Program that would have made tuition free; yet, again, nothing. It was clear to me that University College struggled with a lack of brand awareness within the St. Louis market and an undefined relationship with Washington University. With over a dozen brick and mortar competitors in the region, thousands more online in the marketplace were crowded and noisy. The yearly marketing budget for University College wasn't big enough to outspend the competition, and so I knew we had to find a smarter approach.

The problems facing University College weren't new. Raising brand awareness and finding more students was a common issue facing the modern university, including continuing education divisions. At first, I approached the problem by looking at the conversion attributions of each part of the student journey at the research and discovery stage. Students would request information from the website or attend an open-house night. However, the traditional open-house event relied too heavily on finding one evening that fit into the schedule of a busy adult. Here digital marketing could increase registrations for the event, but it couldn't guarantee attendance would follow. Meanwhile, the website was organically creating the same amount of inquiries each month as an open house. The lack of brand awareness at passive and active exposure stages made the cost of trying to get new students to directly apply for a program and skip inquiring caused diminishing returns. With more than forty programs at University College across multiple levels, there wasn't enough budget to do program-specific search marketing for every program. The solution wasn't going to be found by just addressing the marketing of the student journey.

When the marketing and admission teams started to look at the data side of the student journey, we found the opportunities that were being missed. We had access to enrollment information that was at the end of the journey. So, we could see the demographics of University College's students in individual courses. We hadn't been excluding Washington University employees using tuition benefits for their own education. This meant we were including an audience that wasn't degree-seeking, taking fewer courses per semester, and had irregular enrollment patterns. A better understanding of University College's audience was needed to find new degree-seeking students. We started by building data-driven personalities of our audience, which combined data points from several sources. Website analytics monitored key locations on our website for degree programs, applications, and conversion points. Audience intelligence tools than separated web traffic from these potential students into a variety of demographic, behavioral and psychographic data segments, which was indexed against population size in the St. Louis region and proclivity to convert. From here, we could overlay these segments against first-party data in our application management system and CRM. The resulting personas were the most accurate view of our students to date. This enabled us to find marketing solutions that were better targeted. Messages resonated because it was the right audience, and students were more interested in degree programs we offered. Within just three short years, the enrollment trend was reversed, improving three to four percent across consecutive semesters.[1]

Starting a Data Revolution

No democracy is formed overnight, so neither is one built on data. Starting a data revolution requires more than just having the data points or the understanding of how to use them. It requires alignment that brings together data silos across organizations and stakeholders. It drives purpose towards a meaningful impact to the consumer who is sharing with the organization. Establishing a foundation can be both flexible to any data set for a product or service. Still, it is maintainable without needing unlimited resources.

Just because the marketing department wants the data doesn't mean other departments and their stakeholders are willing or required to share it. While it might make sense in a hierarchy-based organization to just convince the leadership at the top to order other departments to share access to their data silos, this approach rarely finds happy stakeholders in enthusiastic compliance. Stakeholders need to understand the purpose and goal behind building the data democracy together to get buy-in. It is important to remember that stakeholders are not going to simply rely on logical arguments, as fellow human beings would. Instead, it must be an emotional appeal that solidifies the alliance. Stakeholders can't be positioned as losing control of their data silo. How the data flows must give reverence to the sourcing systems and departments.

The purpose behind building a data democracy shouldn't be just to have one or to just collect data with no reason. Every data point should work towards an end goal as the collection for which will require the cooperation and benefit for the consumer. Even if the consumer is not an active contributor to the democracy, once they are aware passively of the collection, their reaction will be based on the perception of who benefits. Should the organization be taking advantage of the arrangement, the consumer might abandon or reject the product or service in the future. Conversely, if the consumer sees the advantage in their favor, they might be less resistant to providing additional data and consider the benefit an extension of the product or service under consideration.

It might sound over the top to consider a constitutional convention as a method in which to establish a foundation for a data democracy. Yet, a project this important to an organization shouldn't be conceived on the back of a napkin after work at the bar. The inclusion of stakeholders will require an agreement that can be reviewed and amended to reach consensus. End goals need quantifiable metrics to measure success that respects the consumer providing data. In this way, they must benefit from an equal member of democracy. The framework should also look to be limited enough in scope to be manageable by all departments involved. This requires a data model that constantly provides feedback and can be responsibly maintained beyond the tenure of the founding department leadership.

VOTE Data Framework Model

Every industry has unique metrics that matter only to their marketing goals, while at the same time, sharing other metrics across different product or service sectors. Rather than attempt to assume which metrics will matter to all marketers and organizations when building a data democracy, a framework model is a better approach. With a model that focuses on what data should mean to an organization, marketers can avoid data overload and useless reports that display only vanity metrics. Therefore a relevant model for data democracy should only contain data that is valuable, organizable, targetable, and explainable (VOTE).

Valuable data is any meaningful and relevant for an organization's goals. Data in this category is the most salient when it can be connected between the consumer and the product or service. The intent here is that not all data is valuable to an organization's, and should be used to make the amount of data manageable for all stakeholders. The discovery of valuable data is possible when its presence is justified by both quantitative and qualitative factors. Does having more of this data improve the model? Does having this data provide insight into the consumer journey or audience? Only data that is positive in both factors should be considered valuable.

Organizable data has the most criteria in the model as it is only data that can be collectible, storable, sortable, and repeatable. Just because marketing wants the data doesn't mean the consumer can or will share it. To be collectible, the consumer must be willing and able to share it. When the consumer shares that data, marketers must have a location to store it for as long as needed. From there, they must be able to sort it in relation to all other data in the model. The collection of the data should be repeatable so that the model remains representative of consumer insights, while always collecting more data points to improve.

Targetable data should be data points within the model used for directly aiming or indirectly knowing that for which consumers aim. The intent is to remove any doubts for marketers about what data is needed or required by this model. Without data that is targetable, nothing in the rest of the model is useful to an organization. Targetable data should answer the who, what, where, when, and why of consumers. At the same time, it provides insight into how to reach them. Marketers having targetable data know that they are including the right data in the model, because again, both the quality of the data and quantity of the data should improve the targeting on the consumer journey.

Explainable data is the criteria that any data used in the model is understood by stakeholders within and outside of marketing. Every organizational hierarchy marketing is accountable to others higher up in leadership, and so, they need to understand why the data is useful to marketing. If the data isn't created or stored by marketing, the other departments need to understand why it is important for marketers to have those data points. This means more than just providing a data definition. The quintessential reason for marketing is to "show their work" to prove that all the data in the model is valuable, organizable and targetable. By taking the time and resources to make sure the data is explainable, the framework for the VOTE model will sustain the data democracy for its duration in support of the organization's products or services.

Responsible Democracy

An often retold story after the Constitutional Convention in the United States was when founding father Benjamin Franklin was asked what type of government had been created. His answer was, "A republic, if you can keep it."[2] A data democracy faces similar challenges. Once it is planned and built, it will need to be maintained. Neglect from mentalities like, "set it and forget it." This will only lead to ruin that can devalue the quality of data and can lessen the quantity of data points available. Therefore, establishing guidelines for data maintenance that includes hygiene, append, purchasing, and unification will help in both keeping this important democracy and enabling it to thrive.

The practice of data hygiene is the maintenance of data points by cleansing unusable and inaccurate data. This helps improve the accuracy and targetability of the data model, increasing its efficiency over time. Marketers familiar with direct mailing tactics have used address hygiene tools from the postal service and certified mail service providers for decades. Email marketing platforms and CRMs have automated controls for similar maintenance and prevention. However, good data hygiene practices shouldn't be limited to just outbound efforts but rather an essential activity within every part of the data model.

It is very likely that not all the data points that are needed will come from a single source. The use of data appending is necessary to join different sources into a single data view. Considerations should be given to what sources of data can overwrite different data points and in what direction will each append occur. Data sources closest to the consumer should have priority while likely also providing improved insight. Caution should be taken when appending, since that might risk the chance of mixing valuable data with irrelevant data points, or that an automated append process might overwrite useful data fields. By following best practices, data appending can enhance data models with greater depth that can widen consumer understanding. Thus, it improves how the overall model is used.

The limit of most data models is what data can be collected from the consumer by the organization, however with data purchasing, third parties can provide an expanded data set from their sources. The important difference between these sources is that while third-party data is aggregated data on a general group of people, first-party data is information the marketer collects directly from the customers like their interactions with the organization. If third-party data lets the marketer reach a broad persona, then first-party data lets them pinpoint a hyper-specific persona.[3] Data models should not rely exclusively on data purchases or data from sources that come from third parties, but rather they are a way to enhance first-party data and data points provided directly from the consumer.

Typically the approach to appending and purchasing data will likely flow in a single direction, while the best approach for any data model should be the unification across all data sources and views. This should allow for the two-way flow of data across all sources in the data model. The optimization that can flow from unification can also improve data hygiene by purging all sources of duplicates and useless data points. This is not to argue that data democracies should start by attempting to gather all the data. Remember the VOTE model, but take the best data points from the best sources together into a unified view of the consumer for personalization.

With the above guidelines in place, an organization has started the process towards establishing data governance. While the term might have a negative connotation for some marketers and communicators not wanting to lose control, the choice is a preemptive move against certain worst-case scenarios. Leandro DalleMule, chief data officer at AIG, and Thomas H. Davenport, President's Distinguished Professor in Management and Information Technology at Babson College, a research fellow at the MIT Initiative on the Digital Economy, and a senior adviser at Deloitte Analytics, writing for the Harvard Business Review points out that, "The importance of investing in data governance and control—even if the payoff is abstract— is more easily understood and accepted if a company has suffered from a major regulatory challenge, a data breach, or some other serious defense-related issue."[4] There are many dangers to any democracy, but addressing these vulnerabilities early with stakeholders builds trust in helping preserve a bright future for a data democracy.

Greetings, Programs!

At this point, marketers and communicators have both what to consider as a framework when starting a data democracy and how to maintain that data model in the best interest of the organization and its stakeholders. The cornerstone that is missing is where the data should go, which data tools should be considered, and how that will impact the consumer. This is becoming more imperative to organizations. In most cases, data is becoming a differentiator because many companies don't have the data they need. Although organizations have measured themselves in systematic ways using generally accepted accounting principles for decades, this measurement has long been focused on physical and financial assets — things and money.[5] And yet, what makes the most powerful platforms Google, Facebook, and Amazon? They all continue to be how they've accumulated, organized, and used their data.

Of course, not every organization has the capacity, resources, and time to emulate the major platforms in building self-sufficient data democracies. However, some platforms are designed to help businesses collect and manage data. Popular customer relationship management (CRM) services like Salesforce and Microsoft Dynamics along with enterprise resource planning (ERP) platforms like Oracle and SAP are widely considered industry leaders in helping organizations manage both products and services with data. Many more CRMs, ERPs, and marketing tools exist. The above brands shouldn't be considered an endorsement of any service over another. But rather, considerations should be given to outside platforms that are designed for these purposes over the internal development of in-house software. Vijay Gurbaxani, Founding Director of the Center for Digital Transformation (CDT) and Taco Bell Endowed Professor of Business and Computer Science at the Paul Merage School of Business, University of California in Irvine writes in the *Harvard Business Review* about the platform economy of how online marketplaces are changing the face of business. He wrote that, "An important consequence of the platform economy is that, other things being equal, bigger players often do better than smaller ones. When a larger business invests in a software platform, the gains accrue from a greater number of customers, employees, or production units, which means that it can justify an investment when a smaller competitor cannot. This means smaller businesses need to build their software platforms for scale right from the start. Since scaling quickly is tough, a smaller business may need to create partnerships or networks to help them grow. Either way, scale becomes a critical part of how companies employ software thinking. Leverage scale if you have it; build for scale if you don't."[6] This means that outside platforms offer better capacity. Scale for organizations from the start struggle in attempting to build in-house software unless that is the product or service the organization is trying to create.

Of course, not all software is created equal. Only true platforms that harness developer ecosystems to create third-party applications that enhance the platform or customization to fit different product and service sectors have the true market advantage in helping organizations build data democracies. This network effect of developers multiplies the impact of a platform that very few organizations can match with in-house developer teams. This is best illustrated with an example scenario, Company A and Company B. Both can both afford to hire five software developers, which according to Glassdoor, makes an average salary of $80,394 per year in 2019.[7] Company A looks to build their data democracy in-house from scratch, while Company B looks to take advantage of an outside platform that uses an ecosystem. Company A and Company B need their software to have five distinct functions. So, Company A hires five developers and assigns a single function to each of them. But now, they are out of developer resources. Meanwhile, Company B uses an ecosystem platform. Instead of hiring five developers, Company B hires only two while saving the other three salary lines. The ecosystem platform includes a community of consultants and developers, in addition to the modest amount of 100 developers working for the platform. This only costs Company B the equivalent of one developer's salary because the platform has other organizational accounts. Company B can also select a consultant agency that specializes in building applications on the platform for their product or service sector. This agency alone has fifteen developers but only costs Company B two developer salaries because the agency can work for other companies in that sector. Company B now has 117 developers working to improve the same five distinct functions with the same cost in developer salaries as Company A that went in-house. Company A will always be limited by the abilities of their five developers, meaning that if they add functions, it either requires an additional developer or less time spent on the existing functions. Meanwhile, Company B can leverage 117 developers to either improve existing functions or expand into new functions. The developers working for the agency and the ecosystem platform also have more incentive to improve and expand functions. It will attract more companies to their platform and services, allowing each to hire more developers. Therefore, organizations that embrace a community-driven approach of internal and external resources are better positioned to achieve cutting-edge data democracy than companies that silo their efforts into a single tribe.

Do Hackers Dream of Electric Sheep?

Cui bono, as the Latin phrase goes, "to whom is it a benefit" is the consideration that every data democracy must answer with a single word response: consumers. As in almost every way, the consumer interacts with a product or service both passively and actively. These activities belong to them. While data isn't currently considered to be the property of an individual, at this moment in time, it is a transaction none the less. Therefore the consumer must benefit from the exchange of data that occurs between them and an organization for the product or service they have sought. The most important way to know if the consumer is benefiting or not is by looking at the product-market fit. The concept of product-market fit began in technology startup culture. Growth hackers pushed the importance as a way to achieve what mattered most to startups that were ready to scale growth. Silicon Valley venture capital, Marc Andreessen, defined product-market fit to mean being in a good market with a product that can satisfy that market.[8] But that leaves the question of how to measure it from the consumer's point of view. GrowthHackers's founder, growth hacking author, and initial head of growth at numerous startups, Sean Ellis, considers product-market fit to be less abstract and measurable by asking a simple question. "I ask existing users of a product how they would feel if they could no longer use the product. In my experience, achieving product-market fit requires at least forty percent of users saying they would be "very disappointed" without your product. Admittedly, this threshold is a bit arbitrary, but I defined it after comparing results across nearly 100 startups. Those that struggle for traction are always under forty percent, while most that gain strong traction exceed forty percent."[9] From this metric and threshold, organizations can have an understanding of their product-market fit. Perhaps the first valuable data point for a growth hacking marketer and communicator to measure.

But what are growth hackers and why are they important to building a data democracy? According to Andrew Chen, the former leader of Uber's Rider Growth product teams and now a venture capitalist, "Growth hackers are a hybrid of marketer and coder, one who looks at the traditional question of *'How do I get customers for my product?'* and answers with A/B tests. They respond with landing pages, viral factor, email deliverability, and Open Graph. On top of this, they layer the discipline of direct marketing, with its emphasis on quantitative measurement, scenario modeling via spreadsheets, and a lot of database queries. If a startup is pre-product-market fit, growth hackers can make sure virality is embedded at the core of a product. After product-market fit, they can help run up the score on what's already working."[10] In essence, they are marketers that have embraced the possibilities of data utilizing skillsets reserved for software developers and engineers in order to enhance their marketing efforts. Perhaps if the data democracy is the engine in an organization's car, then growth hackers are the all-in-one engineer that can build it. They are the salesperson that can sell the car off the lot, and the mechanic that can keep it running for years to come.

Growth hacking is more than just a job title or ability to use code in marketing efforts. It is a mindset. A focus on growth for the product or service that is informed by testing different marketing strategies and tactics, each test showing data points about what worked and what didn't. This testing validates the attribution models that were the framework of data, marketing, and results that were key points of chapter two. Marketers and communicators learning with growth hacking techniques will understand which platforms like search from chapter three, social from chapter four, and/or e-commerce in chapter five. These can provide valuable, organizable, targetable, and explainable data needed in the VOTE model from this chapter. By embracing the "always be testing" philosophy,[11] growth hacking marketers can leverage every stage of The Modern Consumer Decision-Making Journey in chapter six from initial consideration to retention and then perhaps subscription. Because skillsets in marketing don't have to be limited to only writing generic content, the ability to include data in order to use techniques from chapter seven allows for personalization of content at scale. The wherewithal to see the whole board, understand how each piece of data works together, and then use those pieces to execute a strategy growth for the products or services that anticipates the consumers' needs is exactly the kind of talent organizations need to build data democracies.

If You Build It, They Will Come

The concepts behind growth hacking and its utilization of data-driven models can be applied outside of startups to any category. This was true when I used these principles to growth hack UMSL's CRM to increase the student enrollment funnel in 2014. In the years that followed, I improved the university's website as a gateway for converting students and using social media marketing to drive sold-out open house events. The challenge was finding more ways to attract students with a marketing budget that hadn't changed in the five years. The university wasn't going to give us more money for another billboard, radio spot, or digital campaign. We had to find a no-cost solution that would drive more students. But, we also had to understand more of why students chose UMSL. While UMSL asked students in the application process this question, as the car buying experience from chapter two demonstrated, the most common answer of "friend or family" wasn't an attribution that we could model.

At this point, I remembered an article about a survey conducted by the University of California, Los Angeles (UCLA) which looked at over 190,000 first-year students across 238 four-year colleges and universities in the United States called the CIRP Freshmen Survey.[12] That year, UCLA listed the twenty-three reasons for choosing a college that was "very important" in influencing their final college selection. I reviewed the list from the top, looking for some insight into the student's consumer journey of picking a college. The highest four reasons were: the college has a very good academic reputation (63.8 percent), the college's graduates get good jobs (55.9 percent), I was offered financial assistance (45.6 percent), and the cost of attending the college (43.3 percent). None of these was anything the marketing and communication department at a university could impact directly. In fact, it would take any universities years to improve, if they even could. The fifth highest reason caught my eye, a visit to the campus (41.8 percent). We had already maxed out the open house events happening twice a year, but the campus tours were happening multiple times per day, every weekday.

We then started to build our data models looking for the most valuable campus tour related data from several key enrollment sources. We organized the information from the bottom of the funnel and worked up. The application had a campus tour data point that every student was answering. We could sort this data against the CRM of prospective students who were being imported or updated with a campus tour data source as having taken a tour. At the top of the funnel, we had website analytics on the campus tour website. Again, we compared this data to other sources for enrollment to see how often it was present in data records for students. Campus tour ranked sixth on a list of twenty-nine possible CRM touchpoints for UMSL enrolled students over two years, with half of the sources above it being automated touchpoints that every applied or interested student record would already have. It was undeniably a valuable data point. We also had a targetable data point to focus our efforts. We were looking for students who were interested in taking a campus tour to see the university for him or herself. Because we had taken the steps to determine if the campus tour data was valuable, we had organized that data point against all other sources. And because we could target this student from their initial visit to the campus tour website, we had all the criteria for explainable data sets for leadership to sign off on the project.

Still, the data was telling me this wasn't going to be easy. The campus tour website had an eighty-six percent form abandonment rate. Those that completed the form had twenty-five total fields to complete. It was like the Energizer Bunny of forms. It kept going and going, scrolling across three separate full screenshots to capture it all. The easy solution would have been to just make the form shorter. In fact, that move alone could have increased conversion rates, but that wasn't going to solve the problem. The campus tour website needed a better user onboarding experience. It had to allow for personalization, and a way to grow more campus tours from each student visitor.

My team at UMSL looked at user onboarding across a variety of sites, including the social network Twitter, the question and answer site Quora, and a now-defunct group dating website called Grouper. We realized that the best user onboarding experiences didn't have one long form but were split across several steps. On the old form, the student's name and contact info were first while the date of their tour was at the bottom. On the new form, we made this the first step. If the form was abandoned after the first step, we still knew who they were and when they were coming. We could contact them with emails to remind them and also send them back to the form to complete it. The next step helped them personalize their campus tour experience by speaking with an academic advisor, taking tour residence halls, or learn more about extracurricular activities like Greek life. There were over fifty different ways they could create an experience just for their interests. Again, if the student stopped at the second step, we knew who they were, when they were coming, and what they would like to see on campus. The next step in the form was the academic program and mailing address information that allowed for a more tailored communication plan before and after the visit. At this point, the student was completely done with scheduling their tour. Still, the form wasn't done because a hidden bonus step appeared, asking if they wanted to invite up to two friends with them on the tour. One student signing up for a campus tour visit was good but getting three students at the same time was great. At this point, the student could enter basic contact info for their friends and the CRM would begin a communication plan to invite them on a tour with their friend. Now we could map the importance of the "friend or family" data point if we wanted, but more importantly, we had a more valuable personalized campus tour experience.

Within the first three months of the new campus tour website, we saw a thirty-seven percent increase in campus tours. By the end of the year, UMSL had the largest campus tour attendance in school history, without spending a dollar more in marketing. No single data source we used could have helped us reach this outcome. It required a data model that used the most valuable, organizable, targetable, and explainable data points that didn't wait for students to tell us why they chose UMSL. It showed us their vote in the data.

CHAPTER NINE

Privacy in the Era of Data Democracy

One of the most impressive marketing experiences I've had in the era of data democracy is also the most diverse among my peers. Either marketers and communicators are impressed at the cutting-edge use of data or they are creeped out by the invasion of privacy. My point of view is biased as the previous chapters should illustrate. Yet as a victim of identity theft data breaches multiple times, like millions of people every year, I believe we should be mindful of the use of data.

It was the wintertime a few years ago in 2016 when it happened. I was spending most of my weekends doing a variety of home improvement projects both inside and outside. Around the house, I was laying landscaping rock, while at the same time we were preparing to have a new carpet installed inside.

Saturdays and Sundays generally started the same way. I would order the maximum amount of landscaping rock that my car could hold from the local Lowe's home-improvement store, lay the rock down around the house, and repeat. I could do about three or four runs per day before we started any other activities we had planned with our young son. I would order the rock from my smartphone using Lowe's website and would checkout as a guest. Therefore, I didn't have to create a user account. Lowe's website still required an email account for the receipt, which went to my Gmail address that included a Google account.

In preparing to have new carpet installed, one concern that we had was our longtime family cat, Smokie, who had struggled with urinary tract infections for years and occasionally had accidents on the carpet in one part of the house. Not wanting the new carpet in that room stained, the carpet installer suggested we rip up the carpet in that area and spray a product called Kilz on any stains we see on the floor. My wife knew I would be making another run to Lowe's that morning, so she asked me to purchase Kilz while she ripped up the carpet.

I had never used Kilz before and was completely unaware of the product category upon arrival at the local Lowe's. I started my search in the floor clearer area but saw nothing labeled Kilz. There weren't any Lowe's associates in the aisle, and instead of looking for one, I reached for my smartphone and searched for the Kilz product. It was then that I discovered the product was a paint-based primer and was located in the paint aisle. At this point, I closed the browser on my smartphone and headed to the paint aisle. Once there, I quickly located the product. After I purchased the product, I went home and returned to laying rock while my wife used the Kilz on the stains.

Within an hour, I received an email at my Gmail address with the subject line, "Are You Still Shopping for Paint?" from Lowe's.[1] The email contained information about their paint products, available paint brands, and paint tip checklist. At first glance, the subject line and content didn't register with me, but then the marketing side of my brain kicked in. *How did Lowe's do that?* Up to that point, the only Lowe's emails I was receiving were e-receipts from my mobile purchases. I hadn't created a user account on the Lowe's or requested more information when I visited their website. I checked my smartphone browser to confirm that I wasn't logged into my Google account at the time of the mobile search in the store and I never access my Gmail account from the mobile browser. Even my landscaping rock order had occurred in a separate mobile browsing session. How did they connect this mobile search with my email address without a user account (fig. 9.1)?

It was a marketing puzzle that I had to solve. I began by eliminating what it wasn't. It wasn't display, keyword, or social retargeting with an ad exchange. It arrived via email, but it had to at least track where I was on the website. It wasn't shopping cart abandonment because I didn't try to buy the product — just find it in the store, which meant it was tracking abandonment at the page level. It wasn't CRM based because I wasn't logged into the Lowe's website. And, I didn't have an account. Instead, I only had a trail of mobile purchases. What I knew was that every mobile device had a unique device

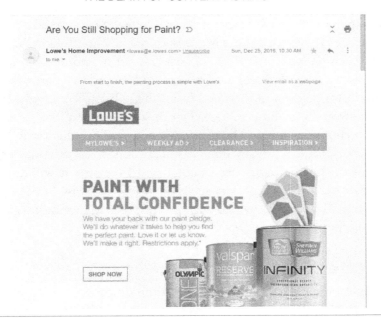

Figure 9.1. Lowes. "Are You Still Shopping for Paint?," Email. December 25, 2016.

identification which can be tracked at the webpage level. I also knew that a mobile ID could be used for cross-device targeting, creating a profile of myself across all websites I visited. Somewhere or somehow on the web, my device had been linked with my Gmail account. So, this likely wasn't something Lowe's built in-house because it included data from other websites they didn't own. Next, I looked at all the advertising and analytics tracking codes on the Lowe's website, eliminating platforms and services with which I was familiar and leaving a handful that I had to research. At the time, I figured that Lowe's was possibly using a collection of services to connect mobile ID with my Gmail account. Then, based on the pages, I was viewing sending product category-based emails through another service for marketing automation that might have completed the link to a stealth account which was created from my previous purchases. Critics might argue that a large retailer like Lowe's has the resources to make this possible, but from my point of view, they were one of the few even trying to put together a complete view of all user data to improve customer experience.

When retelling this story to my peers, the response is usually fifty-fifty, with half of the marketers and communicators being impressed with the use of data in marketing, while the other half believing it crossed a privacy line and consider it creepy. I don't argue with those who disagree because that is their opinion for which they are entitled. For my point of view, I expect to be tracked when I go online. I understand that a large part of search and social platform revenue is from advertising, while e-commerce platforms want to always be selling me a product or service. Therefore, organizations are all trying to figure out how to do it better. This chapter will also not attempt to find the privacy line with data outside of existing regulations that govern specific industries or countries. Likewise, it will not define it but rather explore ways society has to consider it crossed in the past, and how companies have struggled with it more recently them look at a major company that has made privacy a platform.

Don't Be Creepy

It might be said that marketing and communication efforts are a lot like the Central Intelligence Agency covert operations. When it is successful, it is rarely seen, while failure is always public. This is more so in the information age of the internet as mistakes that make the news are there forever. The era of data democracies doesn't correct for this as data is not truth or logic, but rather just ones and zeros of computer code. It isn't infallible either, as both machines and humans makes mistakes. In some cases, unforeseen reactions to the use of data to improve the customer journey and win brand loyalty can have lasting negative impacts.

In 2012, Target wanted to create a marketing engagement opportunity to attract customers who were becoming new parents, even before they might actively create a baby-shower registry in-store or their child's name appears on public birth records. Target already had the data associated with everything a customer purchases. All a customer's purchases are unique to them. This includes how they buy it. Purchased demographic information from third-party sources to compile a holistic customer profile. They also had an analytics department in marketing, working to predict analytics similar to this new child opportunity. According to Andrew Poole, a senior manager in the Guest Marketing Analytics department, the goal was to identify future parents around the second trimester. He told a reporter for the *New York Times Magazine*, "We knew that if we could identify them in their second trimester, there's a good chance we could capture them for years. As soon as we get them buying diapers from us, they're going to start buying everything else too. If you're rushing through the store, looking for bottles, and you pass orange juice, you'll grab a carton. Oh, and there's that new DVD I want. Soon, you'll be buying cereal and paper towels from us, and keep coming back." To find shopping habits that might reveal this stage, he compared the shopping habits of women on Target's baby-shower registry with their due dates they provided the registry. Eventually, he found twenty-five products that produced a "pregnancy prediction" score. Marketing campaigns followed that worked to nudge those with higher scores to purchase baby-related products that exploded revenues and saw Pole promoted. Within a year, however, something happened that made people realize how much data Target had on them. As the *New York Times Magazine* explained, an angry father arrived at his local Target with a coupon mailer for baby clothes addressed to his teenage daughter. He explained his frustration. "She's still in high school, and you're sending her coupons for baby clothes and cribs? Are you trying to encourage her to get pregnant?" The father learned later that evening that his daughter was expecting in a few months. Target knew before him.[2] That was the headline that followed as a massive news barrage and public relations issue was unleashed. Hundreds of news websites and television networks covered the privacy angle of what Target knew before the father did.

Target never apologized. Instead, it insisted it neither broke privacy laws nor did anything wrong. To be clear, they didn't break the law. However, based on the overwhelming amount of negative press at the time, the public zeitgeist viewed it as a violation of privacy. Again, not attempting to place a value judgment on Target's strategy, but a data democracy has to co-exist within the public sphere. Therefore, it's important to prepare for and possibly prevent backlash.

Red Team

Military jargon and strategy are now quite common in businesses and organizations outside of the defense industry. There might be many reasons for this from veterans being more accepted in the workforce and organization leadership based on their experience to numerous publications of Sun Tzu's *Art of War* aimed at non-military professionals. Or, perhaps to quote Don Cheadle's character in *House of Lies* after characters use several military terms, including HALO (high altitude, low opening) to describe a consulting assignment, "Management consultants love that special forces jargon."[3]

One such military strategy that an organization may find useful in preventing backlash from the use of data in marketing is the Red Team concept. Red teaming is the practice of rigorously challenging plans, policies, systems, and assumptions by adopting an adversarial approach. A Red Team may be a contracted external party or an internal group that uses strategies to encourage an outsider perspective.[4] A more common way to think about it is by playing the devil's advocate to take the opposite side and test the validation of defense. By establishing a Red Team, an organization can approach both the collection and use of data points for marketing and communications from the point of view of the user or media.

Perhaps the best way for a Red Team to experience and test for weaknesses in a data-based consumer journey is by giving it data of their own. The Red Team ideally should have very little knowledge, like the consumer would, of how the data points will be used. This allows them to have an unbiased and first-hand reaction to the experience. The Red Team should then be taken through a series of actions and steps. The consumer, likewise, might progress along the same journey, while also testing scenarios from a blank slate of giving it conflicting, improper, or incorrect data points that might lead to unexpected outcomes the marketing and communication teams would not anticipate. If possible, what might happen should the consumer go dark and not give data points? How does the journey, models, and experience change or adapt to that situation?

Finally, the Red Team should present their findings, reactions, and recommendations to both the marketing and communication team, as well as the data governance stakeholders. This would do well to prepare an organization for any possible backlash from the consumer or the news media. Still, even with a Red Team, there is no guarantee that everything the public might object to will be found. However, it is better to be prepared for a public relations storm than be caught unaware and underprepared.

Facebook Under Siege

Even platforms like Facebook aren't immune to public backlash regarding the use of data. Since the United States presidential election in 2016, Facebook has faced tremendous criticism for how it handled user data on the platform. More so once it was revealed that foreign entities used the platform to manipulate voters during the election. In these incidents, it wasn't the organization that so much abused the data from consumers, but how others who had access to the platforms data points using advertising tools manipulated the public.

The onslaught started in March 2018 when *The New York Times*[5] and *The Guardian/Observer*[6] both reported that a political data firm called Cambridge Analytica had used Facebook to harvest the profiles of over fifty million users. Despite the headlines, it wasn't a data breach or exploit that allowed the firm to access the profiles. Instead, Facebook had given third-party application developers on the platform-wide access to user data until 2015. Facebook users themselves were giving up their data by taking a personality quiz created by a different firm with affiliation with Cambridge Analytica, which would scrape some private information from their profiles and those of their friends. Facebook permitted this activity at the time. The only violation from Facebook's point of view was that the firm which created the personality quiz did not abide by the rules of Facebook developers by sharing the information with Cambridge Analytics as a third-party, who then stored it. It was then reported that Cambridge Analytica worked with Republican Party presidential campaigns to perform a variety of services related to target audiences for digital ads fund-raising appeals, and modeling voter turnout. Before the end of 2018, Cambridge Analytica would close down the firm under the public pressure it was facing on numerous fronts. Meanwhile, Facebook changed third-party developer data access.[7]

Perhaps the most damaging abuse of user data on Facebook came from the revelations that the Russian government used the platform to subvert the United States presidential election in 2016. While the news articles on this topic have been numerous, the most official reports from Special Counsel Robert Mueller's investigation[8] and the Senate Select Committee on Intelligence (which published two volumes in July 2019[9] and October 2019[10]) mention Facebook a combined 267 times. It's important to note the Facebook platform wasn't the only site Russian operatives used and the activities went far beyond advertising. They further included computer hacking and disinformation campaigns. However, the criticism in the public sphere from users, news media, and the governments have continued to put Facebook on its heels.[11] Facebook has made repeated efforts to fight foreign interference, increase transparency, and reduce misinformation[12] by combating coordinated inauthentic behavior[13] in an attempt to secure the platform against further maleficence.

Facebook's platform isn't alone in receiving criticisms or being a target for bad actors, whether criminal or state sponsored. The lesson for organizations seeking to create data democracies is to continue to assess and reassess how might the data being collected is being used to cause harm to the consumer if used by a third-party bad actors. Marketers and communicators might be too close to the situation to see possible worst-case scenarios. Therefore, they should seek help from those more experienced in risk management, public relations, and legal fields. Then hopefully organizations can work backward to mitigate the dangers to consumers.

The Walled Garden Approach

If there is a single company that represents the antithesis of everything that a data democracy stands for, it is Apple, Inc. And yet, Apple has built a trillion-dollar platform based on an intersection of technology and privacy. This has been made possible because Apple designs both the hardware and software for their ecosystem. While Apple users can still access the platforms of Google, Facebook, and Amazon on any device Apple makes from either applications or web browsers, Apple purposely designs and limits the access to data from their users from organizations and marketers.

Apple's approach to its ecosystem is often called a "walled garden" in the news media, though it is better defined as a closed platform where access to content in the form of applications and media is restricted to Apple's devices and software. It started with the iPod in 2001, where users could only listen to music legally purchased from Apple's software, the iTunes store. Both iPods and iTunes gained popularity. Capabilities of the content expanded to include movies, television shows, and books. After Apple introduced the iPhone in 2007, they created a store for mobile applications becoming the only effective way users could add third-party software to their devices.[14] For content creators and application developers to access these device users, they must agree to Apple's guidelines and requirements before they are approved in the store. As the exclusive gatekeepers to the walled garden, Apple can maintain control of the platform and the data available within.

Beyond devices and software, Apple has expanded its platform to include services that feature privacy. In March of 2019, Apple introduced three subscription services for news (Apple News+), video (Apple TV+), and video games (Apple Arcade), which have been added to subscriptions for music (Apple Music) and cloud storage (iCloud).[15] Apple devices serve as a gateway to these services, increasing the buy-in from users against alternatives by other platforms and services by offering a single-source provider. Apple users don't have to subscribe to these services for their devices to work, nor does Apple prevent users from subscribing to competing services like Spotify for music or Netflix for video.

While the above services and devices don't compete directly with Google's and Facebook's primary advertising revenue streams in search and social, Apple has put forward alternatives. In search, Apple offers Search Ads exclusive to the Apple App Store based only on keyword data offering no user tracking, no data sharing, and no ads to Apple IDs registered to minors.[16] This keeps smartphone application discovery within the App Store and away from search engines like Google. In social, Apple introduced single sign-on from their Apple IDs called "Sign in with Apple" across their entire ecosystem, including third-party applications. After which they updated their App Store Review Guidelines to require developers to include it if they already made another third-party option for single sign-on available to users.[17] This competes with both Google and Facebook single sign-on offerings, cutting them off from more user data outside their platforms.

Apple isn't shy about promoting its focus on privacy for its platform and devices either. From a giant banner on a Las Vegas building during the CES gadget show in January 2019 proclaiming, "What happens on your phone stays on your phone." A play on the popular Las Vegas marketing catchphrase, "What happens in Vegas, stays in Vegas." Television ads for the iPhone during the World Series in 2019 that state more personal data exists on a person's smartphone than in their home from their location, messages, heart rate after a run, and more private personal things that should belong to the user.[18] This isn't to state that a data democracy cannot exist within Apple's walled garden. In fact, many already do, but they have to abide by Apple's rules when operating within a closed platform. Rules that can change at any time without warning.

This Is Why We Can't Have Nice Things

Concerns about privacy can and should exist within organizations looking to build a data democracy. Governments around the world have and continue to express concerns about the amount of data that companies collect from consumers. The United States has an array of federal regulations like the CAN-SPAM Act to establish rules for commercial emails, the National Do Not Call Registry to block telemarketers, and the Children's Online Privacy Protection Act to require privacy policies on websites for the protection of children under the age of thirteen as well as other regulations specific to certain industries like Health Insurance Portability and Accountability Act (HIPAA) in healthcare and Family Educational Rights and Privacy Act (FERPA) in higher education. As data breaches, foreign interference, and other malicious activities grow in frequency and damage. The impact to legitimate data collection efforts will only be more scrutinized and regulated. A new class of laws are coming into effect that have a sweeping impact on the relationship organizations. These can have with consumer data online. The European Union's General Data Protection Regulation (GDPR) in 2018 and the California Consumer Privacy Act that went into effect in 2020 are mandating that consumers have more direct control over their data. These new regulations require organizations to disclose what data is being collected, allow consumers to access that data, and allow the option to either correct or delete data as they choose.[19] Additional protections exist within these regulations that are designed to curb the collection of data without a lawful basis for processing the data like their consent, under contract, a legal obligation, vital or legitimate interests, and public tasks.[20] More importantly, companies are prohibited from discriminating against consumers who opt out of data collection and must still provide them with free services to an extent.[21] The seismic shift of these data protection laws will have an impact outside of states and country borders. Organizations are more likely to holistically apply data protection standards instead of siloing the information based on their consumer's location.

This era will also likely test the ethics of many organizations as consumer trust hangs in the balance. Former advertising executive Richard Stokes had such a moment, before he left the advertising industry, after watching a startup demo a map of San Francisco with a red line tracking a real, anonymous person throughout their day. He was challenged to infer what could be known about her. She left the house at 7 a.m., went to Starbucks, went to a school, went to a yoga studio, and then went back to the school. She was a mother with at least one child, and he knew where she lived. He knew this because this woman's cell phone was tracking her every move.[22] The abuse of trust may not hurt Target's quarterly reports or Facebook's monthly active users for extended periods of time, but if public opinion collectively shifts against using personal data, the impact to organizations that rely on these data points will be felt like the meteor that killed the dinosaurs.

This is why such importance was placed on experience, strategy, and relevance within a data democracy. Chapter six showed this with post-evaluation, post-engagement, and personal experience stages centered on the consumer reaction to the experience of the product or services. Chapter seven made the point that strategy is key to the development of personalization of dynamic content around techniques like association, visitation, connection, recommendation, and location. Then, from chapter eight, when looking at building a data democracy, only the most relevant data that follows the VOTE model of valuable, organizable, targetable, and explainable data points should be collected. If the voice of the consumer can be found in data, be sure it is used to find a better way before it becomes a scream and the law to be left alone.

CHAPTER TEN

What's Next for the Data Democracy

The last thing I enjoy doing is writing about the future state of marketing and communications. Not because the future is unpredictable; in fact, I might end up being wrong. I hate it if I get it right. That was what I was asked by the chair of my graduate advising committee, Dr. Gary R. Hicks, professor of Mass Communications at Southern Illinois University Edwardsville, for the conclusion of my thesis on fake blogs in 2010.

At the time, I was writing about how several commercial companies had created a series of fake blogs and the public reaction to them. The first few attempts by Sony and Wal-Mart were outed by the news media as fake attempts to sell products. Sony PlayStation Portable was fake blogged to children. Wal-Mart faked a couple RVing across America visiting their stores to improve public perception about employee treatment. A successful attempt was a movie marketing campaign for *Forgetting Sarah Marshall* in 2008 that included a fabricated network of blogs, fan pages, a music rockstar, and a faked television show called *Crime Scene: Scene of the Crime*. It was located on the NBC website next to their real network shows. The news media didn't react to these fake websites the same way as they did Sony and Wal-Mart. There was also no consumer reaction or rejection from the market either. The movie even had a loosely connected sequel: *Get Him to the Greek*.

I then wrote that the fabricated frameworks of fake blogs created an unstable relationship between the consumer and the reality of their surroundings. It seemed impossible to prevent or protect consumers from fake content like blogs or websites. Worse yet, because they were easy to create, the potential expansion was enormous. They became restricted only by the resources, knowledge, and alliances available to those creating fake content. Those with power or influence could create massive fabricated frameworks so complex they might defy any attempt by the average consumer to deconstruct for authenticity. I predicted that consumers would likely find themselves under siege by fake content with more nefarious objectives then the purchase of a movie ticket.[1]

The Russian government's election interference efforts during the United States presidential election in 2016 were my worst fears come true. As news reports trickled out, revelation after another, government reports showed a sophisticated and well-funded effort to create fake content across social networks with hundreds of messages and fake accounts. As a marketing and communications professional, I understood the potential influence of these efforts. Not everyone agreed. Nate Silver, election statistician and editor-in-chief of *FiveThirtyEight* viewed them as agnostic to traditional election forces.[2] Facebook CEO Mark Zuckerberg's initial reaction was to say, "It is a 'pretty crazy idea' to think that fake content could have an impact on the election."[3] I wasn't alone in my personal assessment either. Information warfare expert Molly McKew wrote the Russian campaign was designed to game the algorithms behind the social networks, while appearing as authentic American voices pushing out elaborate themes stoking psychological divisions. A number of instances lead to an impact where events and demonstrations were organized by Russians posing as Americans on social media.[4]

Of course, fake content, whether created by individuals, organizations, or foreign powers, is already in a negative context because it is fake. Perhaps it was easier to predict the potential for a larger negative for fake content because it flowed from a negative already. Data, however, is logically neutral. It is neither negative or positive at first, where only the application can be bad or good. So, that is how I'll approach this final chapter and the future state of the union for data democracy looking at how certain trends might be bad or good, while considering both uncertainty and user trust.

The Content Wars 2: Streaming Edition

A trend that could be a bad future for data democracies is the embargo of content by organizations that produce and distribute it. They war with each other for consumer attention. This was Michael H. Goldhaber's main observation when he wrote in 1997 about the attention economy. The global economy shifted away from material-based economies to one based on the capacity of human attention. Since many services online were offered for free, they were offered in exchange for the currency of users paying attention.[5] Platforms benefited the most from this exchange, while media organizations responsible for content struggled to adapt.

In this book, Netflix has been an example of an organization that has embraced data to scale and grow subscribers. Netflix's growth, however, along with early streaming platforms like Hulu and Amazon Prime Video, and the advance of digital technology to many any size screen and device, has upended the traditional media networks as people choose cord cutting as a way to escape cable companies and broadcast television providers. As of 2018, the number of streaming subscribers around the world (613 million) surpassed the number of cable subscribers (556 million) for the first time, according to the Motion Picture Association of America. This shift has been followed by every major media organization following the attention of audiences as WarnerMedia, owned by AT&T, introduced HBO Now, HBO Go, and HBO Max services. Comcast, the owner of NBCUniversal, has been bleeding its twenty-one million cable subscribers. It has announced Peacock for 2020; and the entertainment juggernaut Disney launched its streaming service in 2019 called Disney+ including movies and television content from Disney, Pixar, Marvel, Star Wars, National Geographic, Hulu (Disney is now the majority stakeholder), and ESPN.[6]

The list of companies competing with independent streaming platforms has the potential to rival the hundreds of channel numbers in a cable package as each tries to grab monthly paying subscribers. Several platforms are also in this competition Google with YouTube TV, Apple with AppleTV+ and Amazon with Amazon Prime Video. Some of these organizations are taking the opposite approach of cable and broadcast television when it comes to allowing advertising within their streaming services. These closed subscribers-only streaming services, like Disney+, represent perhaps the last attempt of the content kings seeking to repel the open platforms. With them, everything data democracies should cherish about making data available. If some of these streaming services hoard their data behind their paid walls, small and medium-size organizations that don't create movies or television shows would be left without access to promote their products or services with online video advertising to subscription-only audiences. This is troubling because ninety percent of consumers already prefer video to help them make a purchasing decision according to Social Media Today.[7] Likewise, ninety-seven percent of marketers agree that it helps consumers understand products according to Hubspot.[8] An estimate of the web's future by Cisco is that, by 2021, eighty percent of all traffic will consist of video.[9] If this streaming trend continues, it could mean audiences are at multiple services. As a result, audiences become even more fragmented and leaving less for other data democracy marketers to target. Some may even become unreachable as they choose only closed platform devices like Apple with a selection of closed streaming services providers. This leaves only those users without access to premium technology and paid services, making small and medium organizations more reliant on dominant platforms in search, social, and e-commerce to reach their audiences.

This trend does not prevent organizations without streaming services from building data democracies. It only prevents some of the audiences they want to reach to be unavailable on certain services, some of the time. It is also extremely unlikely for any streaming video services or paid-subscription content provider to have 100 percent of internet users as an audience at any point in the future. This means that the future of the internet will remain free. Data will always find a way to be available for those organizations that need it to provide better products and services to their consumers.

Good Morning Hal

Artificial Intelligence (AI) is no longer just a futuristic word reserved for science fiction media but is already transforming the technology landscape, including marketing and communications in a good way. Studies in this field have been going on for decades. Progress has evolved from rule-based systems to machine-learning algorithms, deep-learning methods, and natural language processing. While the public has been watching the news of AI machines beating human world champions at chess and Go for years, now AI machines are beating professional video game players at complex strategy games such as Dota 2 and StarCraft 2. The development of a commercial AI arms race is ongoing within all the major platforms like Google, Facebook, and Amazon as well as technology and software companies like Microsoft, IBM, and Salesforce to name just a few. In turn, there has been a rise of AI-powered marketing applications in startups like Adgorithms AI engine that autonomously optimizes paid media channels, Cognitiv who uses deep learning to automatically create custom ad buying algorithms, Kenshoo, and Lattice Engines that uses collective learnings to power lead generation software.[10]

What this means for organizations in the era of data democracies is that marketers and communicators will have access to AI-powered tools to gather, organize, and analyze data. It will become less incumbent on organizations to have to build the entire toolset to run a data democracy internally as third-party services operate interchangeably or are controlled at a central hub by AI-powered intelligences that seek to maximize programmed results. On the machine-learning front, Google Analytics introduced Automated Insights in 2016. Google's AI machine intelligence finds key insights from among the thousands of metric and dimension combinations that can be reported offering relevant insights about audience activity and recommendations.[11] The advantage to organizations is that these recommendations are based on their actual audience's activities and not just generic one-size-fits-all suggestions. By the nature of being machine-learning, it can increase efficiency over time as more data is made available and improvements are made.

The dynamic content personalization discussed in chapter seven is possible with the right utilization of data and marketing tools networked together. However, the usefulness of the data for personalization will depend on the ability of the organization to learn anytime from the collected data to make almost real-time personalization suggestions. This is where the inclusion of deep learning could perhaps overcome both the hurdles of collecting enough data and creating this kind of hyper-personalization according to Michael Brenner, author and the CEO of Marketing Insider Group. In addition to deep-learning use cases in real-time bidding software for buying ad space and the automatic generative of translation, copy, and image captions.[12]

Technology, data, and marketing is most likely to be forever changed by AI is the use of natural language processing, where AI can take human input from voice and text then provide an output based on the query. Amazon's use of Alexa to act as a shopping assistant and smart home hub, from chapter five, is just one example using voice as other platforms have released their own natural language processing efforts with Google Assistant and Apple's

Siri. While on Facebook, bots responding to text input have become the go-to messenger solution for customer service and retail. When considering that messaging is so important to Facebook's ambitious, from chapter four, it's easy to see how these can be integrated across local services and universally available. As natural language processing with AI evolves and the simplicity of interaction reduces friction, it is possible to imagine a future where data is made available to the platform assistants and bots from organizations. It removes the burden or requirement to maintain separate mobile applications leaving only a few platforms and websites.[13] Consumers will be faced with AI technology that understands them. They can learn to anticipate them, and feels like it was personalized exclusively for them.

In many ways, organizations are already seeing the inclusion of AI in their data democracy efforts. So, the future may already be here. The benefit is that AI technologies can only hope to improve upon their impact both in technology as a means and consumers as their users. When looking to include AI, marketers and communicators should remember what was discussed in chapter eight about building a data democracy. The approach of "set it and forget it" can only lead to ruin. Marketers and communicators might not be expected to understand the coding behind machine-learning algorithms, deep-learning methods, or natural language processing. They will still need to understand the outcomes, because AI is only as powerful as the data it uses. Therefore, marketers and communicators should understand the data, the consumer journey, and goals before allowing AI to assume any responsibility of what to do with it.

There Can Be Only One

The future, however, is always uncertain, since predictions can never fully anticipate the vast amount of change that advancement in technology can bring. Consider that the previous channels of mass media before the internet were limited to the broadcasting of content. Therefore, in the early days of the internet, the observational bias would also just be a channel for content, as Bill Gates predicted, likely felt certain to those at the time. Artificial intelligence's natural language processing is showing the potential to shift the underlying interaction of consumers with technology paving the way for potentially voice-only operating systems and platforms. Already market analyst firms like ComScore are reporting that, by 2020, more than half of all smartphone users will be engaging with voice search technology.[14] Data will continue to play a role in this new future but the unknown is whether access to this data will still form a democracy. Today's major platforms are in a technology arms race to have the most powerful AI voice interactions.

The difference in this technology shift relies on those who will be the responsible gatekeepers of knowledge. Platforms have chosen data-powered algorithms to determine the information for billions of people. However, the removal of display screens and the limitation of voice-only responses, as Amazon's Alexa was shown to do in chapter five, creates the challenge of limited answers to every question. What happens when there is no search engine result page for websites on Google or products on Amazon to review and select from? As author James Vlahos explored in his book on voice computing, it is the concept of position zero. The one short answer will become the most daunting challenge for organizations in this new era. Platforms are already building knowledge graphs to answer simple fact-based questions like: *Where is Big Ben?* or *Who is the president of France?*[15] This leaves the last hopes of content marketers whispering words to the wind as platforms continue their control and dominance.

In what way will organizations and marketers be able to use the data from this future era of technology? As they did before in their respective areas, platforms like Amazon and Google have begun to open their ecosystems to applications for users to "talk" with or act as API to power the voice interface. From Matt Ward's perspective by owning the interaction, accumulating data and controlling the customer experience, these platforms can insert themselves into each and every value-chain. They do this by gathering a little piece of data from every organization.[16] Organizations can try to resist this incursion into their respective and protective areas; however, as news, publishers, and entertainment media discovered in trying to restrict their content, users will simply go somewhere for what they need. The risk of not being available and accessible is that a competitive organization can replace in order to provide the interactions for which users are asking.

This is why for marketers understanding both consumer intent and their decision-making journey will continue to be critical as new technology develops. Every interaction with voice from users is still data that will need to be tracked. Platforms will still need to provide access to these voice-only users for organizations in order to better user experiences, outcomes and revenue in order to continue to improve themselves over time. As long as the data that organizations receive, from chapter two, continues to be targetable with an affordable price and provides accountability with results, voice-only technology will be valuable to marketing for products and services.

Worlds Built on Data

It is the beginning of a new dawn to building a better world from data. It won't be easy or simple. It won't be fast or cheap. To be good, it must be hard. Content cannot build this better world. It tried and failed. There was too much of it, endless and valueless without data to guide it. Only data gives content any value. In doing so, data has replaced content as the most important element to an organization.

The lessons from this book about data show that with it the value of marketing can be proven. From data, marketers and communicators can determine what drives consumers to a product or service, without relying on the consumer to remember how or why it happened. This knowing of the attributions of each marketing channel comes choices. The true voice of consumers, data registered and recorded accurately, votes for their preference. The freedom of the internet, and the low barrier of entry into the distribution of content compared to previous media, saw the transfer of power from the creation of content to platforms that could algorithmically use data. Once consumers didn't have to pay for it, they become users and the product of the platforms for marketers.

From platforms, the truth is in the data. From search, what keywords were used become data points. What did they search with as a device becomes a data point, and where did they search as location becomes a data point? Social friends have become a data point, interests have become a data point, and how people interact with everyone and anything is a data point. From the marketplace, the wants and needs of consumers are a data point. The more that is purchased, the more reliance is built on a single source and builds more data points, with both buyer and seller. Essentially, the data points run in a continuous flywheel loop. Google, Facebook, and Amazon have mastered and dominated data to become the leading platforms of this new era. And yet, because the user is the product, they require organizations to leverage the data that they make available, to advertise and market within. By sharing data the platforms hope to improve, the experience of both the user and the organization in a symbiotic relationship with neither the user, the organizations marketing their products or services, or the platform that hosts can function without them.

Consumer choice doesn't occur in a vacuum. It is a journey, a path that has been studied for more than a decade. With data, that journey can now be mapped for all the complexities and stages that exist for the modern consumer. However, only data can provide the stages of the consumer along this journey, even in real-time. Marketing and communication professionals can now target their messages and channels along that journey because of data. By using The Modern Consumer Decision-Making Journey, connecting each stage with relevant data points, messages, and channels an organization can do more than brand awareness and lead generation to market its products or services by creating experiences that establishes connection and engagement which enables consumer loyalty.

By using data, content doesn't have to be static because one-size-fits-all. It can be dynamic, speaking to every consumer as if the marketing is speaking to each of them one at a time. This requires the content to adapt to the data it is given and be driven by more personalization based on the association, visitation, connection, recommendation, and location of the consumer. Of course, this doesn't happen all at once. Still, content can scale with data-based personalization. This is possible already as different organizations in different industries have found how to build dynamic content from data to improve their products or services, and the marketing that feeds the continuous innovation.

There are no secrets to building a data democracy. It doesn't require only one specific technology or vendor to unlock. To build it requires teamwork, across an organization with vested stakeholders who believe in the value of the data that will be shared across silos. To know that the right data is found, it should fit within the VOTE framework model containing only data that is valuable, organizable, targetable, and explainable. Once built, a data democracy must be maintained based on guidelines to be always useful to an organization. A data democracy also doesn't have to be built alone. Third-party applications can be utilized to assist but not control data within an organization. The last piece of building this better tomorrow requires that data must have a purpose. The product or services that use the data must fit within the lives of the consumers that have given the data.

Organizations must remember that, when using data, everyone is watching them, and may not forgive them if misused. Data given by people, either intentionally or unintentionally. It can be used in ways both positively and negatively. It may be used in ways that violate a personal perception of privacy or the laws that govern its use. If organizations want to continue to collect and use data, they must not be blind to what could go wrong, but rather be aware and prepared to face the public backlash if they break consumer trust.

Those that support content as king would have everyone believe that content can be built like the pyramids of ancient Egypt to stand forever. These believers in content forget that the pharaohs are no more, their empire gone, and their language of hieroglyphs is just content for archaeologists and historians to study. They should recall the final lines of *Ozymandias*, the poem by Percy Bysshe Shelley, in which he describes the antique land of that time.

> *"My name is Ozymandias, King of Kings;*
> *Look on my Works, ye Mighty, and despair!*
> *Nothing beside remains. Round the decay*
> *Of that colossal Wreck, boundless and bare*
> *The lone and level sands stretch far away."*[17]

From content, no kingdom that lasts can be built. Consider the point that from the very essay that was titled, "Content is King." If it was still salient and fundamental to success, it wouldn't have been removed from Microsoft's website.

The future potential of data is not limited to science fiction. It is here, today, and all around us. Tomorrow will bring new technologies and ways to use data that are unforeseen. However, the marketers that take up the charge to create a data democracy will be the founding fathers and mothers to a legacy from which their organization will benefit. From these new data democracies, a wealth of knowledge will be built that is more valuable than any kingdom on Earth.

AUTHOR'S NOTE

August 23, 2020

I'm done. The two worst words in the English language for any author, because every book has to end, while the world around it keeps moving forward. In the days and months since I've prepared this book for publication, not a day has gone by that I haven't read a news story, marketing research, or a data case study that should have been in this book.

The world has changed in unimaginable ways with the dual pandemic and economic crises of 2020. I observed organizations undergoing fundamental paradigm shifts in how they interacted with consumers in this new era. What determined the survival of the fittest for many organizations was their strength in data. The most dominant of which continues to be the search, social, and e-commerce platforms.

Benjamin Franklin once wrote that, "Well done is better than well said." While the death of content is here, the story of data continues. There is much more to say on that topic. I invite you to come along with me at my author's website www.deathofcontent.com to wherever the journey takes us.

ACKNOWLEDGMENTS

Writing is a solitary endeavor, but no author works in a vacuum. It takes a circle of trusted friends and supportive family members to help craft a book. I was blessed to have more than my fair share of both in this endeavor.

First and foremost, my wife Iris and son Meyer, where spending time is filled with love, laughter, and the joy of reading. To my family: Mom, Dad, and Aunt Brenda for letting me explore while always having my back. For my grandparents and Uncle Bill, whose memories are a blessing. To the friend whom I consider as close as family, Levi Locke, whose friendship during every mutual struggle and success has only strengthened our bond. Thank you all.

Perhaps more than she'll ever know, I'm grateful for my friend Alexis Nugent, who edited every chapter's first drafts. She acted as a sounding board for ideas. Muse during the days and weeks of writer's block, and, above all else, Alexis believed that I had something to add to the discussion... way before I did.

I thank Mark Michael for permission to use his Modern Decision-Making Journey model. Along with his constructive comments and insightful recommendations to help make the book more approachable.

My intellectual debt is to Andrew Perry and Rosie Walker at mediate.ly.

Their dedication to data-based marketing and data analysis matched me at every turn. I believe true partners will always challenge you to be better.

I am especially grateful to Elizabeth Tucker, who gave an extraordinary amount of time, priceless guidance, and warm encouragement. She reminded me that we learn from stories, and those stories are what hold our attention.

To Chris Schafer and everyone at Tactical 16 Publishing, thank you for helping veteran authors like me tell their stories to the world.

NOTES

Chapter One – The King is Dead

1. Opened in 1991 as the Alton Belle Casino.
2. Gates, "Content Is King."
3. Steinberg, "S. H. Five Hundred Years of Printing."
4. Smulyan, "Selling Radio: The Commercialization of American Broadcasting,"
5. Galbi, "U.S. Advertising Expenditure Data – Purple Motes."
6. See "Hyperlink Advertising Explodes on the World Wide Web."
7. D'Angelo, "Happy Birthday, Digital Advertising!"
8. Ha, "EMarketer Predicts Digital Ads Will Overtake Traditional Spending in 2019."
9. Internet Live Stats, "Number of Internet Users."
10. "WorldWideWebSize.Com | The Size of the World Wide Web (The Internet)."
11. Bodnar, "Marketers: This Is Why We Can't Have Nice Things."
12. "Our Story | HubSpot - Internet Marketing Company."
13. Hall, "Top of Mind: Use Content to Unleash Your Influence and Engage Those Who Matter To You," 151.

14. Bodnar, "Marketers: This Is Why We Can't Have Nice Things."

15. Lacoste, "WTF Is Micro-Moment Marketing?"

16. Egan, "Opinion | The Eight-Second Attention Span."

17. Schaefer, "Content Shock: Why Content Marketing Is Not a Sustainable Strategy."

18. Kornbluth, "Who Needs America Online?"

19. Walker, "Every Day Big Data Statistics – 2.5 Quintillion Bytes of Data Created Daily."

20. "The World's Most Valuable Resource Is No Longer Oil, but Data."

21. Author's note: References to Alphabet Inc. going forward will be labeled as Google instead of the conglomerate parent company.

22. Auletta, "How the Math Men Overthrew the Mad Men."

23. Paine, "Common Sense: The Origin and Design of Government."

Chapter Two – Living in the Data Democracy

1. Rheinlander,"Everything You Wanted to Know About Marketing Attribution Models (but Were Afraid to Ask)."

2. Inter-Parliamentary Union, ed. "Democracy: Its Principles and Achievement."

3. Quigley, "Constitutional Democracy."

4. Young,"Ogilvy on Advertising in the Digital Age."

5. Gershgorn, "The Internet Can't Handle Functioning like a Democracy."

6. Leonsis, "How Tech Has Led the Evolution of Media and a Glimpse at What's to Come."

7. Internet Usage & Social Media Statistics, "Internet Live Stats."

8. Thompson, "The Print Apocalypse of American Newspapers."

9. Shatzkin, "A Changing Book Business: It All Seems to Be Flowing Downhill to Amazon."

10. Herrman, "Mutually Assured Content."

11. Serra, Richard, and Clara Weyergraf, "Richard Serra: Interviews, Etc. 1970-1980."

12. Leonard, "How Netflix Is Turning Viewers into Puppets."

13. Morris, "Netflix Is Now Bigger Than Cable TV."

Chapter Three – A Platform by Any Other Name

1. Ward, "Why Is Amazon the Most Powerful Platform in the World?"

2. StatCounter Global Stats, "Search Engine Market Share Worldwide."

3. Google Search. "Google's Search Algorithm and Ranking System."

4. SEO Book. "How Does Google Rank Websites & Other Content in Their Search Results?"

5. Broder, "A Taxonomy of Web Search."

6. Coldewey, "Google, Rome, and Empire."

7. Bodnar, "Marketers: This Is Why We Can't Have Nice Things."

8. Sullivan, "Post-PRISM, Google Confirms Quietly Moving To Make All Searches Secure, Except For Ad Clicks."

9. Edwards, "Is SEO Dead? - ClickZ."

10. Shih, "AdWords: Google Search Partners List 2019."

11. Johnson, "What Is the Google Display Network?"

12. Clifford, "Leftover Ad Space? Exchanges Handle the Remnants."

13. Modena, "Google Shopping Campaigns Guide: Best Practices, Tips & Tricks."

14. Lister, "37 Staggering Video Marketing Statistics for 2018."

15. McAlone, "Teens Watch More Netflix and YouTube than TV - Business Insider."

16. Google Ads Help, "About Video Ad Formats."

17. Smith, "Google Ads Keyword Planner: What Has Changed (And How To Use It)."

18. Google Ads Help, "About Keyword Matching Options."

19. Lavidge and Steiner, "A Model for Predictive Measurements of Advertising Effectiveness."

20. Gossen and Hinderliter, "Bursting the Branded Search Bubble."

21. Blake, Nosko, and Tadelis, "Consumer Heterogeneity and Paid Search Effectiveness: A Large Scale Field Experiment."

22. Kim, "Dear EBay, Your Ads Don't Work Because They Suck."

23. Rey, "Yes, Google Punished EBay for Bad SEO Practices, but It Wasn't Part of 'Panda' Update."

24. Blake, Nosko, and Tadelis, "Consumer Heterogeneity and Paid Search Effectiveness: A Large-Scale Field Experiment," 155-174.

25. Gannes, "Ten Years of Google Maps, From Slashdot to Ground Truth."

26. BuiltWith, "Mapping Technologies Web Usage Distribution."

27. StackShare, "Bing Maps API vs Google Maps vs Mapbox | What Are the Differences?"

28. iDatalabs, "Companies using Google-Maps."

29. Ingraham, "Apple: YouTube App Will Not Be Included in IOS 6, Google Working on Standalone Version."

30. Nickinson, Dobie, and Hildenbrand, "How Nexus, Samsung, and Apple Drove Android's Evolution."

31. Nieva, "Google Maps Has Now Photographed 10 Million Miles in Street View - CNET."

32. O'Beirne, "Google Maps's Moat."

33. Popular Mechanics, "101 Gadgets That Changed The World."

34. We Are Social, "Percentage of All Global Web Pages Served to Mobile Phones from 2009 to 2018."

35. Gannes, "Ten Years of Google Maps, From Slashdot to Ground Truth."

36. Young, "Location Based Geo-Targeting Boosts Paid Search Ad Performance...Or Does It?"

37. D'Onfro, "New Ads in Google Maps Will Try to Get You to Stop for Gas or Eat at McDonald's."

38. Chait, "Half the Money I Spend on Advertising Is Wasted; the Trouble Is I Don't Know Which Half."

Chapter Four – It's a Social World After All

1. Facebook Investor Relations, "Facebook - Resources."

2. Global Policy Forum, "What Is a 'Nation'?"

3. Constine, "2.5 Billion People Use at Least One of Facebook's Apps."

4. World Population Review, "China Population 2019 (Demographics, Maps, Graphs)."

5. Instagram for Business, "Instagram Business."

6. WhatsApp, "About WhatsApp."

7. We Are Social, "Most Popular Global Mobile Messenger Apps as

of October 2019, Based on Number of Monthly Active Users (in Millions)."

8. Boyd, "The History of Facebook: From BASIC to Global Giant."

9. Hill, "'People You May Know:' A Controversial Facebook Feature's 10-Year History."

10. Ibid.

11. Ibid.

12. Backstrom, "People You May Know."

13. Allen, "How Popular Is Facebook vs Twitter vs Instagram vs Snapchat vs Pinterest?"

14. Wong, "Facebook Overhauls News Feed in Favor of 'Meaningful Social Interactions.'"

15. Boyd, "The History of Facebook: From BASIC to Global Giant."

16. Wu, "The Attention Merchants: The Epic Scramble to Get Inside Our Heads."

17. Madrigal, "The Fall of Facebook."

18. Yeung, "Facebook: 60 Million Businesses Have Pages, 4 Million Actively Advertise."

19. Madrigal, "The Fall of Facebook."

20. Hale, "What You Think You Know About the Web Is Wrong."

21. Manson, "Facebook Zero: Considering Life After the Demise of Organic Reach."

22. Ward, "Data, Not Privacy, Is the Real Danger."

23. Koch, "The 80/20 Principle: The Secret to Achieving More with Less."

24. Ward, "Data, Not Privacy, Is the Real Danger."

25. Lanchester, "You Are the Product."

26. Facebook Ads Help Center, "About Custom Audiences from Customer Lists."

27. Cohen, "Facebook Officially Launches Lookalike Audiences."

28. Samuelson, "3 Benefits to Using Facebook's Value-Based Lookalikes."

29. Madrigal, "The Fall of Facebook."

30. Finn, "Facebook Relevance Score: 4 Key Facts to Know."

31. Manson, "Facebook Zero: Considering Life After the Demise of Organic Reach."

32. Facebook Investor Relations, "Facebook Reports Fourth Quarter and Full Year 2018 Results."

33. Bras, "[INFOGRAPHIC] Online Overload – It's Worse Than You Thought."

34. Facebook for Developers, "Overview - Facebook Login - Documentation."

35. Peterson, "Facebook Owns Social Login Scene, But Google's Creeping Up."

36. Thompson, "Messaging: Mobile's Killer App."

37. Herrman, "Why Facebook Had To Have WhatsApp."

38. See "WeChat's World, WeChat's World."

39. Bhattacharya, "Facebook Tides over Fake News, Data Privacy to Boom in India."

40. Warzel, "Facebook Isn't Sorry — It Just Wants Your Data."

41. Wilson, "Make-A-Wish Greater Bay Area: Miles' Wish to Be Batkid."

42. Association, Author The ALS, "Understanding the Impact of the Ice Bucket Challenge on The ALS Association's Finances."

Chapter Five – The Everything You Didn't Know You Needed Store

1. Bhasin and Lambert, "The Long, Hard, Unprecedented Fall of Sears." Bloomberg.Com, May 8, 2017. https://www.bloomberg.com/news/articles/2017-05-08/the-long-hard-unprecedented-fall-of-sears.

2. Kapner, Rizzo, and Biswas, "Sears to Stay Open After Edward Lampert Prevails in Bankruptcy Auction."

3. ScrapeHero, "How Many Products Does Amazon Sell? – April 2019,"

4. Bhattacharyya, "Pressured by Amazon, Retailers Are Experimenting with Dynamic Pricing."

5. See Amazon. "Amazon Echo (2nd Generation) — Alexa Speaker."

6. See Amazon. "All-New Kindle - Now with a Built-in Front Light - Amazon Official Site."

7. See Amazon. "Amazon.Com: Sonos One (Gen 1) - Voice Controlled Smart Speaker with Amazon Alexa Built-in (Black): Home Audio & Theater."

8. See Amazon. "Amazon.Com: BOOX Nova Pro 7.8 E-Reader, Front Light, Flush Glass Screen, 2G 32G Support Upgrade to Android 9.0

Soon: Home Audio & Theater."

9. See Amazon. "Amazon's Top Customer Reviewers."

10. See Amazon. "Amazon.Com - Amazon Vine Program."

11. See CNBC, "Jeff Bezos 1999 Interview on Amazon before the Dotcom Bubble Burst,"

12. Mercer, "Amazon PPC Ultimate Guide: How to Advertise Your Products 2018."

13. Zaczkiewicz, "Study Reveals Amazon at 'Center' of Customer Shopping Journey."

14. Richter, "Amazon Passes 100 Million Prime Members in the U.S."

15. Ali, "Amazon Prime Day 2019 Analysis in 8 Charts."

16. Griswold, "Amazon Wants to Replace Free Two-Day Shipping with Free One-Day Shipping."

17. Zaczkiewicz, "Study Reveals Amazon at 'Center' of Customer Shopping Journey."

18. Enright, "Amazon's Growth Accelerates."

19. Dzieza, "Dirty Dealing in the $175 Billion Amazon Marketplace."

20. Lincoln, "Considering Amazon Fulfillment Options? Here Is How To Decide."

21. Wilke, "Virtuous Cycle."

22. Stone, "The Everything Store: Jeff Bezos and the Age of Amazon."

23. White, "The Ultimate Guide to Amazon Advertising."

24. Dzieza, "Dirty Dealing in the $175 Billion Amazon Marketplace."

25. Fischer, "E-Commerce Is Upending Madison Avenue, Led by Amazon."

26. Nagaraj, "A Beginners Guide to Amazon Product Display Ads With Benefits."

27. White, "The Ultimate Guide to Amazon Advertising."

28. Salkever, "Amazon Has a Massive New Division—and No One's Paying Attention to It."

29. Martineau and Matsakis, "Why It's Hard to Escape Amazon's Long Reach."

30. Iqbal, "Twitch Revenue and Usage Statistics (2019)."

31. Castillo, "Some Advertisers Are Moving Half of Their Search Budget

from Google to Amazon, Say Ad Industry Sources."

32. Mull, "There Is Too Much Stuff."

33. Galloway, "This Technology Kills Brands."

Chapter Six – Targeting the Consumer's Journey

1. See National Association for College Admission Counseling, "2017 STATE OF COLLEGE ADMISSION."

2. Lewis, "St. Elmo. Financial Advertising."

3. Court, Elzinga, Mulder, and Vetvik, "The Consumer Decision Journey | McKinsey."

4. Michael, "The Modern Consumer Decision-Making Journey."

5. McLuhan and Fiore, "The Medium Is the Massage."

6. McKinsey & Company, "Thinking inside the Subscription Box: New Research on e-Commerce Consumers."

7. Hogg, "Customer Journey Mapping: The Path to Loyal Customers."

Chapter Seven – Personalization at Scale

1. Harress, "The Sad End Of Blockbuster Video: The Onetime $5 Billion Company Is Being Liquidated As Competition From Online Giants Netflix And Hulu Prove All Too Much For The Iconic Brand."

2. See Study Lib. "Blockbuster Rewards Membership Guide."

3. Epstein, "Hollywood's New Zombie The Last Days of Blockbuster."

4. Jackson, "The Netflix Prize: How a $1 Million Contest Changed Binge-Watching Forever."

5. Zak, "Alaska's Last 2 Blockbuster Stores Are Closing, Leaving Just One in the U.S."

6. See Omniconvert, "What Is Dynamic Content? Definition & Examples."

7. See Experian, "Mosaic USA Consumer Lifestyle Segmentation by Experian."

8. Harshman, "The Homepage Is Dead: A Story of Website Personalization."

9. Debois, "6 Great Examples of Personalization in Social Media Marketing."

10. Aufray, "14 Referral Marketing Examples To Make You Inspired."

11. Alcántara, "How These 4 Brands Are Using Their Apps to Personalize Customer Experience."

12. Anderson, "How Dynamic Content Makes Your Marketing a Helluva Lot More Personal."

13. Norton, "Fanatics Revamps Cloud Platform, Addressing the Online Unpredictability of Sports Fandom."

14. Taylor, "Fanatics Scores 27,000 Personalized Marketing Campaigns With Salesforce."

15. Murphy, "You Might Not Have Heard of Fanatics yet—but It's Taking over Sports Apparel One League at a Time."

16. Lawrence, "An Exclusive View Inside Fanatics' Email Marketing Strategy."

17. Graser, "Epic Fail: How Blockbuster Could Have Owned Netflix."

18. Plummer, "This Is How Netflix's Top-Secret Recommendation System Works."

19. Baldwin, "Netflix Gambles on Big Data to Become the HBO of Streaming."

Chapter Eight – Building a Data Democracy

1. Gauen, "Serving Adult Consumers of Knowledge."

2. Beeman, "Perspectives On The Constitution: A Republic, If You Can Keep It."

3. Girard, "First-Party Data: How You Can Optimize Your Ads Targeting By Relying On Yourself."

4. DalleMule and Davenport, "What's Your Data Strategy?"

5. Beck and Libert, "The Machine Learning Race Is Really a Data Race."

6. Gurbaxani, "You Don't Have to Be a Software Company to Think Like One."

7. See Glassdoor, "Salary: Developer."

8. Andreessen, "The Pmarca Guide to Startups, Part 4: The Only Thing That Matters."

9. Ellis, "The Startup Pyramid."

10. Chen, "Growth Hacker Is the New VP Marketing."

11. Taparia, "5 Things You Can Learn About 'Growth Hacking' From The Man Who Coined The Term."

12. Morse, "Freshmen Students Say Rankings Aren't Key Factor in College Choice."

Chapter Nine – Privacy in the Era of Data Democracy

1. See Lowes, "Are You Still Shopping for Paint?"

2. Duhigg, "How Companies Learn Your Secrets."

3. Hopkins, "Amsterdam." House of Lies.

4. Rouse, "What Is Red Teaming? - Definition from WhatIs.Com."

5. Rosenberg, Confessore, and Cadwalladr, "How Trump Consultants Exploited the Facebook Data of Millions."

6. Cadwalladr, and Graham-Harrison, "Revealed: 50 Million Facebook Profiles Harvested for Cambridge Analytica in Major Data Breach."

7. Goldhill, "A 'big Data' Firm Sells Cambridge Analytica's Methods to Global Politicians, Documents Show."

8. Mueller III, "Report on the Investigation into Russian Interference in the 2016 Presidential Election."

9. See Senate Select Committee on Intelligence, "Russian Active Measures Campaigns and Interference in 2016 U.S. Election: Volume 1."

10. See Senate Select Committee on Intelligence, "Russian Active Measures Campaigns and Interference in 2016 U.S. Election: Volume 2."

11. Thompson and Vogelstein, "15 Months of Fresh Hell Inside Facebook."

12. Rosen, Harbath, Gleicher, and Leathern, "Helping to Protect the 2020 US Elections."

13. Gleicher, "Coordinated Inauthentic Behavior Explained."

14. Murphy, "Apple's 'Walled Garden' Approach to Content Has Paid off Massively."

15. Lakshmanan, "Apple's Big Services Push Is Starting to Pay Off."

16. See Apple Search Ads, "Apple Search Ads and Privacy."

17. Lakshmanan, "Apple's Privacy-Focused Features Risk Trapping Users in Its Walled Garden."

18. Sullivan, "Apple Gets All Moody in New Privacy Ad for World Series."

19. Kingson and Kokalitcheva, "The Future of Privacy Starts in California."

20. See Focal Point Insights, "9 Examples of Lawful Basis for Processing under the GDPR."

21. Kokalitcheva, "California's New Privacy Law Takes Effect."

22. Stokes, "I Left the Ad Industry Because Our Use of Data Tracking Terrified Me."

Chapter Ten – What's Next for the Data Democracy

1. Hinderliter, "These Words Are Not My Own: Understanding the Frames of a Fake Blog."

2. Silver, "How Much Did Russian Interference Affect The 2016 Election?"

3. Manjoo, "On Russian Meddling, Mark Zuckerberg Follows a Familiar Playbook."

4. Mckew, "Did Russia Affect the 2016 Election? It's Now Undeniable."

5. Goldhaber, "The Attention Economy and the Net."

6. Barnes, "Netflix Was Only the Start: Disney Streaming Service Shakes an Industry."

7. Ahmad, "The State of Video Marketing in 2018 [Infographic]."

8. Hayes, Adam. "The State of Video Marketing in 2019 [New Data]."

9. See "Cisco Visual Networking Index: Forecast and Trends, 2017–2022."

10. Joe, "The Marketer's Guide To Artificial Intelligence."

11. Noyes, "Google Analytics Just Got a New AI Tool to Help Find Insights Faster."

12. Brenner, "How Deep Learning Will Drive The Future of Marketing."

13. Kojouharov, "This Is How Chatbots Will Kill 99% of Apps."

14. Engleson, "The Future of Voice From Smartphones to Smart Speakers to Smart Homes."

15. Vlahos, "Talk to Me: How Voice Computing Will Transform the Way We Live, Work, and Think."

16. Ward, "Product to Platform — Inside Amazon's Dominance."

17. Shelley, "Shelley's Poetry and Prose: Authoritative Texts."

BIBLIOGRAPHY

About Facebook. "Company Info." Accessed December 5, 2019. https://about.
fb.com/company-info/.

About Facebook. "Facebook Unveils Facebook Ads," November 6, 2007.
https://about.fb.com/news/2007/11/facebook-unveils-facebook-ads/.

Ahmad, Irfan. "The State of Video Marketing in 2018 [Infographic]." Social
Media Today, March 6, 2018. https://www.socialmediatoday.com/news/
the-state-of-video-marketing-in-2018-infographic/518339/.

Alcántara, Ann-Marie. "How These 4 Brands Are Using Their Apps to
Personalize Customer Experience." AdWeek, February 19, 2018. https://
www.adweek.com/digital/4-brands-explain-how-their-apps-improve-
customer-experience/.

Ali, Fareeha. "Amazon Prime Day 2019 Analysis in 8 Charts." Digital Commerce
360, July 30, 2019. https://www.digitalcommerce360.com/article/amazon-
prime-day-data/.

Allen, Robert. "How Popular Is Facebook vs Twitter vs Instagram vs Snapchat
vs Pinterest?" Smart Insights, April 7, 2017. https://www.smartinsights.com/
social-media-marketing/social-network-landscape-chartoftheday/.

Amazon. "All-New Kindle - Now with a Built-in Front Light - Amazon
Official Site." Accessed December 6, 2019. https://www.amazon.com/dp/
B07DLPWYB7.

Amazon. "Amazon Echo (2nd Generation) — Alexa Speaker." Accessed

December 6, 2019. https://www.amazon.com/dp/B06XCM9LJ4/.

Amazon. "Amazon.Com - Amazon Vine Program." Accessed December 6, 2019. https://www.amazon.com/gp/vine/help.

Amazon. "Amazon.Com: BOOX Nova Pro 7.8 E-Reader, Front Light, Flush Glass Screen, 2G 32G Support Upgrade to Android 9.0 Soon: Home Audio & Theater." Accessed December 6, 2019. https://www.amazon.com/BOOX-Nova-Pro-Reader-Android/dp/B07L95KPFM/.

Amazon. "Amazon.Com: Sonos One (Gen 1) - Voice Controlled Smart Speaker with Amazon Alexa Built-in (Black): Home Audio & Theater." Accessed December 6, 2019. https://www.amazon.com/gp/product/B074XLMYY5.

Amazon. "Amazon's Top Customer Reviewers." Accessed December 6, 2019. https://www.amazon.com/reviews/top-reviewers.

Anderson, Meghan Keaney. "How Dynamic Content Makes Your Marketing a Helluva Lot More Personal." *HubSpot*, September 10, 2012. https://blog.hubspot.com/blog/tabid/6307/bid/33566/how-dynamic-content-makes-your-marketing-a-helluva-lot-more-personal.aspx.

Andreessen, Marc. "The Pmarca Guide to Startups, Part 4: The Only Thing That Matters." *blog.pmarca.com*, June 25, 2007. http://web.archive.org/web/20070701074943/http://blog.pmarca.com/2007/06/the-pmarca-gu-2.html.

Apple Search Ads. "Apple Search Ads and Privacy." Accessed December 6, 2019. https://searchads.apple.com/privacy/.

Association, Author The ALS. "Understanding the Impact of the Ice Bucket Challenge on The ALS Association's Finances." *The Official Blog of The ALS Association* (blog), June 5, 2019. https://alsadotorg.wordpress.com/2019/06/05/understanding-the-impact-of-the-ice-bucket-challenge-on-the-als-associations-finances/.

Aufray, Jonathan. "14 Referral Marketing Examples To Make You Inspired." *Growth Hackers* (blog), October 3, 2017. https://www.growth-hackers.net/referral-marketing-examples/.

Auletta, Ken. "How the Math Men Overthrew the Mad Men." *The New Yorker*, May 21, 2018. https://www.newyorker.com/news/annals-of-communications/how-the-math-men-overthrew-the-mad-men.

Backstrom, Lars. "People You May Know." Presented at the SIAM AN10 Minisymposium on Analyzing Massive Real-World Graphs, July 12, 2010. http://graphanalysis.org/SIAM-AN10/01_Backstrom.pdf.

Baldwin, Roberto. "Netflix Gambles on Big Data to Become the HBO of Streaming." *Wired*, November 29, 2012. https://www.wired.com/2012/11/netflix-data-gamble/.

Barnes, Brooks. "Netflix Was Only the Start: Disney Streaming Service Shakes an Industry." *The New York Times*, November 10, 2019, sec. Business. https://www.nytimes.com/2019/11/10/business/media/Disney-Plus-streaming.html.

Beck, Megan, and Barry Libert. "The Machine Learning Race Is Really a Data Race." *MIT Sloan Management Review*, December 14, 2018. https://sloanreview.mit.edu/article/the-machine-learning-race-is-really-a-data-race/.

Beeman, Richard. "Perspectives on the Constitution: A Republic, If You Can Keep It - National Constitution Center." *National Constitution Center*. Accessed December 6, 2019. https://constitutioncenter.org/learn/educational-resources/historical-documents/perspectives-on-the-constitution-a-republic-if-you-can-keep-it.

Bhasin, Kim, and Lance Lambert. "The Long, Hard, Unprecedented Fall of Sears." *Bloomberg.Com*, May 8, 2017. https://www.bloomberg.com/news/articles/2017-05-08/the-long-hard-unprecedented-fall-of-sears.

Bhattacharya, Ananya. "Facebook Tides over Fake News, Data Privacy to Boom in India." *Quartz India*, June 23, 2019. https://qz.com/india/1651034/facebook-tides-over-fake-news-data-privacy-to-boom-in-india/.

Bhattacharyya, Suman. "Pressured by Amazon, Retailers Are Experimenting with Dynamic Pricing." *Digiday* (blog), February 21, 2019. https://digiday.com/retail/amazon-retailers-experimenting-dynamic-pricing/.

Blake, Tom, Chris Nosko, and Steven Tadelis. "Consumer Heterogeneity and Paid Search Effectiveness: A Large Scale Field Experiment." *Working Paper*. National Bureau of Economic Research, May 2014. https://doi.org/10.3386/w20171.

Bodnar, Kipp. "Marketers: This Is Why We Can't Have Nice Things." *HubSpot Blog*, July 18, 2017. https://blog.hubspot.com/marketing/marketers-this-is-why-we-cant-have-nice-things.

Boyd, Joshua. "The Facebook Algorithm Explained and How to Work It." *Brandwatch*, January 2, 2019. https://www.brandwatch.com/blog/the-facebook-algorithm-explained/.

———. "The History of Facebook: From BASIC to Global Giant." *Brandwatch*, January 25, 2019. https://www.brandwatch.com/blog/history-of-facebook/.

Bras, Tom Le. "[INFOGRAPHIC] Online Overload – It's Worse Than You Thought." *Dashlane Blog*, July 21, 2015. https://blog.dashlane.com/infographic-online-overload-its-worse-than-you-thought/.

Brenner, Michael. "How Deep Learning Will Drive The Future of Marketing." *Marketing Insider Group* (blog), January 16, 2019. https://

marketinginsidergroup.com/artificial-intelligence/how-deep-learning-will-drive-the-future-of-marketing/.

Broder, Andrei. "A Taxonomy of Web Search." *SIGIR Forum 36*, no. 2 (September 2002): 3–10. https://doi.org/10.1145/792550.792552.

BuiltWith. "Mapping Technologies Web Usage Distribution," February 7, 2019. https://trends.builtwith.com/mapping.

Cadwalladr, Carole, and Emma Graham-Harrison. "Revealed: 50 Million Facebook Profiles Harvested for Cambridge Analytica in Major Data Breach." *The Guardian*, March 17, 2018, sec. News. https://www.theguardian.com/news/2018/mar/17/cambridge-analytica-facebook-influence-us-election.

Castillo, Michelle. "Some Advertisers Are Moving Half of Their Search Budget from Google to Amazon, Say Ad Industry Sources." *CNBC*, October 8, 2018. https://www.cnbc.com/2018/10/08/google-search-losing-some-adverrtising-business-to-amazon-ad-sources.html.

Chait, Gerald. "'Half the Money I Spend on Advertising Is Wasted; the Trouble Is I Don't Know Which Half.'" *B2B Marketing*, May 18, 2015. https://www.b2bmarketing.net/en/resources/blog/half-money-i-spend-advertising-wasted-trouble-i-dont-know-which-half.

Chen, Andrew. "Growth Hacker Is the New VP Marketing." *@andrewchen* (blog), April 27, 2012. https://andrewchen.co/how-to-be-a-growth-hacker-an-airbnbcraigslist-case-study/.

"Cisco Visual Networking Index: Forecast and Trends, 2017–2022." *White Paper*. Cisco, February 27, 2019. https://www.cisco.com/c/en/us/solutions/collateral/service-provider/visual-networking-index-vni/white-paper-c11-741490.html.

Clifford, Stephanie. "Leftover Ad Space? Exchanges Handle the Remnants." *The New York Times*, July 28, 2008, sec. Media. https://www.nytimes.com/2008/07/28/business/media/28adco.html.

CNBC. "Jeff Bezos 1999 Interview on Amazon before the Dotcom Bubble Burst," July 13, 1999. https://www.cnbc.com/video/2019/02/08/jeff-bezos-1999-interview-on-amazon-before-dotcom-bubble-burst.html.

Cohen, David. "Facebook Officially Launches Lookalike Audiences." *AdWeek*, May 19, 2013. https://www.adweek.com/digital/lookalike-audiences/.

Coldewey, Devin. "Google, Rome, and Empire." *TechCrunch* (blog), December 22, 2009. http://social.techcrunch.com/2009/12/22/google-rome-and-empire/.

Constine, Josh. "2.5 Billion People Use at Least One of Facebook's Apps." *TechCrunch* (blog), July 25, 2018. http://social.techcrunch.com/2018/07/25/

facebook-2-5-billion-people/.

Court, David, Dave Elzinga, Susan Mulder, and Ole Jørgen Vetvik. "The Consumer Decision Journey | McKinsey." *McKinsey Quarterly*, June 2009. https://www.mckinsey.com/business-functions/marketing-and-sales/our-insights/the-consumer-decision-journey.

DalleMule, Leandro, and Thomas H. Davenport. "What's Your Data Strategy?" *Harvard Business Review*. Accessed December 6, 2019. https://hbr.org/2017/05/whats-your-data-strategy.

D'Angelo, Frank. "Happy Birthday, Digital Advertising!" *AdAge*, October 26, 2009. https://adage.com/article/digitalnext/happy-birthday-digital-advertising/139964.

Debois, Stefan. "6 Great Examples of Personalization in Social Media Marketing." *The Mention Blog* (blog), February 17, 2019. https://mention.com/blog/personalization-social-media-marketing/.

D'Onfro, Jillian. "New Ads in Google Maps Will Try to Get You to Stop for Gas or Eat at McDonald's." *Business Insider*, May 24, 2016. https://www.businessinsider.com/google-expands-promoted-pins-in-maps-2016-5.

Duhigg, Charles. "How Companies Learn Your Secrets." *The New York Times*, February 16, 2012, sec. Magazine. https://www.nytimes.com/2012/02/19/magazine/shopping-habits.html.

Dzieza, Josh. "Dirty Dealing in the $175 Billion Amazon Marketplace." *The Verge*, December 19, 2018. https://www.theverge.com/2018/12/19/18140799/amazon-marketplace-scams-seller-court-appeal-reinstatement.

Edwards, Andrew. "Is SEO Dead? - ClickZ." *ClickZ*, July 14, 2014. https://www.clickz.com/is-seo-dead/30610/.

Egan, Timothy. "Opinion | The Eight-Second Attention Span." *The New York Times*, January 22, 2016, sec. Opinion. https://www.nytimes.com/2016/01/22/opinion/the-eight-second-attention-span.html.

Ellis, Sean. "The Startup Pyramid." *Startup Marketing*. Accessed December 6, 2019. https://www.startup-marketing.com/the-startup-pyramid/.

eMarketer. "EMarketer Releases New Global Media Ad Spending Estimates," May 7, 2018. https://www.emarketer.com/content/emarketer-total-media-ad-spending-worldwide-will-rise-7-4-in-2018.

Engleson, Susan. "The Future of Voice From Smartphones to Smart Speakers to Smart Homes." *Comscore, Inc.*, December 15, 2017. https://www.comscore.com/Insights/Presentations-and-Whitepapers/2017/The-Future-of-Voice-From-Smartphones-to-Smart-Speakers-to-Smart-Homes.

Enlyft. "Google-Maps Commands 93.01% Market Share in Web Mapping," February 7, 2019. https://enlyft.com/tech/products/google-maps.

Enright, Allison. "Amazon's Growth Accelerates." *Digital Commerce 360*, December 23, 2015. https://www.digitalcommerce360.com/2015/12/23/amazons-growth-accelerates/.

Epstein, Edward Jay. "Hollywood's New Zombie The Last Days of Blockbuster." *Slate Magazine*, January 9, 2006. https://slate.com/culture/2006/01/the-last-days-of-blockbuster.html.

Experian. "Mosaic USA Consumer Lifestyle Segmentation by Experian." Accessed December 6, 2019. http://www.experian.com/marketing-services/consumer-segmentation.html.

Facebook Ads Help Center. "About Custom Audiences from Customer Lists." Accessed December 5, 2019. https://www.facebook.com/business/help/341425252616329.

Facebook for Developers. "Overview - Facebook Login - Documentation." Accessed December 5, 2019. https://developers.facebook.com/docs/facebook-login/overview/.

Facebook Investor Relations. "Facebook - Resources." Accessed December 5, 2019. https://investor.fb.com/resources/default.aspx.

Facebook Investor Relations. "Facebook Reports Fourth Quarter and Full Year 2018 Results," January 30, 2019. https://investor.fb.com/investor-news/press-release-details/2019/Facebook-Reports-Fourth-Quarter-and-Full-Year-2018-Results/default.aspx.

Finn, Allen. "Facebook Relevance Score: 4 Key Facts to Know." *WordStream*, August 23, 2019. https://www.wordstream.com/blog/ws/2017/09/14/facebook-relevance-score.

Fischer, Sara. "E-Commerce Is Upending Madison Avenue, Led by Amazon." *Axios*, April 23, 2019. https://www.axios.com/ecommerce-data-marketing-amazon-google-12c1615a-4a85-40b7-bf3d-2d741f18f3e9.html.

Focal Point Insights. "9 Examples of Lawful Basis for Processing under the GDPR," February 21, 2018. https://blog.focal-point.com/9-examples-of-lawful-basis-for-processing-under-the-gdpr.

Galbi, Douglas. "U.S. Advertising Expenditure Data – Purple Motes." Blog, September 14, 2008. https://www.purplemotes.net/2008/09/14/us-advertising-expenditure-data/.

Galloway, Scott. "This Technology Kills Brands." YouTube, June 1, 2017. https://youtu.be/BXEu8RcneZQ.

Gannes, Liz. "Ten Years of Google Maps, From Slashdot to Ground Truth." *Recode*, February 8, 2015. https://www.vox.com/2015/2/8/11558788/ten-years-of-google-maps-from-slashdot-to-ground-truth.

Gates, Bills. "Content Is King." Internet Archive - Microsoft.com, January 3,

1996. http://web.archive.org/web/20010126005200/http:/www.microsoft. com/billgates/columns/1996essay/essay960103.asp.

Gauen, Claire. "Serving Adult Consumers of Knowledge." *The Ampersand*, April 25, 2019. https://artsci.wustl.edu/ampersand/serving-adult-consumers-knowledge.

Gershgorn, Dave. "The Internet Can't Handle Functioning like a Democracy." *Quartz*, November 8, 2018. https://qz.com/1422925/the-public-internet-was-almost-a-democracy/.

Girard, Alex. "First-Party Data: How You Can Optimize Your Ads Targeting By Relying On Yourself." *HubSpot Blog*, October 11, 2018. https://blog. hubspot.com/marketing/first-party-data.

Glassdoor. "Salary: Developer," October 1, 2019. https://www.glassdoor.com/ Salaries/developer-salary-SRCH_KO0,9.htm.

Gleicher, Nathaniel. "Coordinated Inauthentic Behavior Explained." *Facebook Newsroom* (blog), December 6, 2018. https://about.fb.com/news/2018/12/ inside-feed-coordinated-inauthentic-behavior/.

Global Policy Forum. "What Is a 'Nation'?" Accessed December 5, 2019. https://www.globalpolicy.org/nations-a-states/what-is-a-nation.html.

Goldhaber, Michael H. "The Attention Economy and the Net." *First Monday* 2, no. 4 (April 7, 1997). https://doi.org/10.5210/fm.v2i4.519.

Goldhill, Olivia. "A 'big Data' Firm Sells Cambridge Analytica's Methods to Global Politicians, Documents Show." *Quartz*, August 14, 2019. https:// qz.com/1666776/data-firm-ideia-uses-cambridge-analytica-methods-to-target-voters/.

Google Ads Help. "About Keyword Matching Options," December 11, 2019. https://support.google.com/google-ads/answer/7478529?hl=en.

Google Ads Help. "About Video Ad Formats." Accessed December 5, 2019. https://support.google.com/google-ads/answer/2375464?hl=en.

Google Search. "Google's Search Algorithm and Ranking System." Accessed December 5, 2019. https://www.google.com/search/howsearchworks/ algorithms/.

Gossen, Ron, and Jon Hinderliter. "Bursting the Branded Search Bubble." *Currents*, October 2013.

Graser, Marc. "Epic Fail: How Blockbuster Could Have Owned Netflix." *Variety* (blog), November 12, 2013. https://variety.com/2013/biz/news/epic-fail-how-blockbuster-could-have-owned-netflix-1200823443/.

Griswold, Alison. "Amazon Wants to Replace Free Two-Day Shipping with Free One-Day Shipping." *Quartz*, April 25, 2019. https://qz.com/1605167/

amazon-to-make-free-one-day-shipping-standard-on-prime/.

Gurbaxani, Vijay. "You Don't Have to Be a Software Company to Think Like One." *Harvard Business Review*, April 20, 2016. https://hbr.org/2016/04/you-dont-have-to-be-a-software-company-to-think-like-one.

Ha, Anthony. "EMarketer Predicts Digital Ads Will Overtake Traditional Spending in 2019." *TechCrunch* (blog), February 20, 2019. http://social.techcrunch.com/2019/02/20/emarketer-digital-ad-forecast/.

Hale, Tony. "What You Think You Know About the Web Is Wrong." *Time*, May 9, 2014. https://time.com/12933/what-you-think-you-know-about-the-web-is-wrong/.

Hall, John. *Top of Mind: Use Content to Unleash Your Influence and Engage Those Who Matter To You.* 1st ed. New York: McGraw-Hill Education, 2017.

Harress, Christopher. "The Sad End Of Blockbuster Video: The Onetime $5 Billion Company Is Being Liquidated As Competition From Online Giants Netflix And Hulu Prove All Too Much For The Iconic Brand." *International Business Times*, December 5, 2013. https://www.ibtimes.com/sad-end-blockbuster-video-onetime-5-billion-company-being-liquidated-competition-1496962.

Harshman, Cara. "The Homepage Is Dead: A Story of Website Personalization." *Moz*, May 2, 2017. https://moz.com/blog/homepage-personalization.

Hayes, Adam. "The State of Video Marketing in 2019 [New Data]." *HubSpot Blog*. Accessed November 14, 2019. https://blog.hubspot.com/marketing/state-of-video-marketing-new-data.

Herrman, John. "Mutually Assured Content." *The Awl*, July 30, 2015. https://www.theawl.com/2015/07/mutually-assured-content/.

———. "Why Facebook Had To Have WhatsApp." *BuzzFeed News*, February 19, 2014. https://www.buzzfeednews.com/article/jwherrman/why-facebook-was-so-terrified-of-whatsapp.

Hill, Kashmir. "How Facebook Figures Out Everyone You've Ever Met." *Gizmodo*, November 7, 2017. https://gizmodo.com/how-facebook-figures-out-everyone-youve-ever-met-1819822691.

———. "'People You May Know:' A Controversial Facebook Feature's 10-Year History." *Gizmodo*, August 8, 2018. https://gizmodo.com/people-you-may-know-a-controversial-facebook-features-1827981959.

Hinderliter, Jon. "These Words Are Not My Own: Understanding the Frames of a Fake Blog." Graduate Thesis, Southern Illinois University Edwardsville, 2011.

Hogg, Stuart. "Customer Journey Mapping: The Path to Loyal Customers." *Think with Google*, February 2018. https://www.thinkwithgoogle.com/

marketing-resources/experience-design/customer-journey-mapping/.

Hopkins, Stephen. "Amsterdam." *House of Lies*. Showtime, n.d.

"Hyperlink Advertising Explodes on the World Wide Web." Press Release. Palo Alto: FocaLink Media Services, Inc., 1995. Archived 2011-07-18 at the Wayback Machine. https://web.archive.org/web/20110718154139/http://www.zinman.com/images/FocalinkPressRelease.JPG.

Ingraham, Nathan. "Apple: YouTube App Will Not Be Included in IOS 6, Google Working on Standalone Version." *The Verge*, August 6, 2012. https://www.theverge.com/2012/8/6/3223775/apple-youtube-ios6.

Instagram for Business. "Instagram Business." Accessed December 5, 2019. https://business.instagram.com/.

Internet Live Stats. "Number of Internet Users." Accessed December 20, 2018. https://www.internetlivestats.com/internet-users/.

Internet Usage & Social Media Statistics. "Internet Live Stats." Accessed October 3, 2018. https://www.internetlivestats.com/.

Inter-Parliamentary Union, ed. *Democracy: Its Principles and Achievement*. Geneva: Inter-parliamentary Union, 1998.

Iqbal, Mansoor. "Twitch Revenue and Usage Statistics (2019)." *Business of Apps*, February 27, 2019. https://www.businessofapps.com/data/twitch-statistics/.

Jackson, Dan. "The Netflix Prize: How a $1 Million Contest Changed Binge-Watching Forever." *Thrillist*, July 7, 2017. https://www.thrillist.com/entertainment/nation/the-netflix-prize.

Joe, Ryan. "The Marketer's Guide To Artificial Intelligence." *AdExchanger*, October 25, 2016. https://adexchanger.com/data-exchanges/marketers-guide-ai-marketing-advertising/.

Johnson, Tara. "What Is the Google Display Network?" *Tinuiti* (blog), June 13, 2017. https://tinuiti.com/blog/paid-search/google-display-network/.

Kapner, Suzanne, Lillian Rizzo, and Soma Biswas. "Sears to Stay Open After Edward Lampert Prevails in Bankruptcy Auction." *Wall Street Journal*, January 16, 2019, sec. Business. https://www.wsj.com/articles/sears-to-stay-open-after-edward-lampert-prevails-in-bankruptcy-auction-11547636823.

Kim, Larry. "Dear EBay, Your Ads Don't Work Because They Suck." *WordStream*, July 23, 2018. https://www.wordstream.com/blog/ws/2013/03/13/dear-ebay-its-not-adwords-its-you.

Kingson, Jennifer, and Kia Kokalitcheva. "The Future of Privacy Starts in California." *Axios*, September 13, 2009. https://www.axios.com/california-privacy-law-national-impact-8e86bffe-af22-4966-92ff-f44e12aae9d6.html.

Koch, Richard. *The 80/20 Principle: The Secret to Achieving More with Less.*

Reprint edition. New York: Currency, 1999.

Kojouharov, Stefan. "This Is How Chatbots Will Kill 99% of Apps." *Chatbots Life*, November 22, 2016. https://chatbotslife.com/this-is-how-chatbots-will-kill-99-of-apps-2fd938a22c99.

Kokalitcheva, Kia. "California's New Privacy Law Takes Effect." *Axios*, January 1, 2020. https://www.axios.com/california-new-privacy-law-effective-3a843f4a-1521-4e33-a20e-f2e1f8803e4d.html.

Kornbluth, Jesse. "Who Needs America Online?" *The New York Times Magazine*, December 24, 1995. http://movies2.nytimes.com/books/98/08/02/specials/aol-mag.html.

Lacoste, Jonathan. "WTF Is Micro-Moment Marketing?" *Inc.com*, January 22, 2016. https://www.inc.com/jonathan-lacoste/wtf-is-micro-moment-marketing.html.

Lakshmanan, Ravie. "Apple's Big Services Push Is Starting to Pay Off." *The Next Web*, May 1, 2019. https://thenextweb.com/business/2019/05/01/apples-big-services-push-is-starting-to-pay-off/.

———. "Apple's Privacy-Focused Features Risk Trapping Users in Its Walled Garden." *The Next Web*, June 4, 2019. https://thenextweb.com/apple/2019/06/04/apples-privacy-focused-features-risk-trapping-users-in-its-walled-garden/.

Lanchester, John. "You Are the Product." *London Review of Books*, August 17, 2017.

Lavidge, Robert J., and Gary A. Steiner. "A Model for Predictive Measurements of Advertising Effectiveness." *Journal of Marketing 25*, no. 6 (1961): 59–62. https://doi.org/10.2307/1248516.

Lawrence, Marta. "An Exclusive View Inside Fanatics' Email Marketing Strategy." *Salesforce Blog*, June 20, 2016. https://www.salesforce.com/blog/2016/06/email-marketing-strategy-fanatics.html.

Leonard, Andrew. "How Netflix Is Turning Viewers into Puppets." *Salon*, February 1, 2013. https://www.salon.com/2013/02/01/how_netflix_is_turning_viewers_into_puppets/.

Leonsis, Ted. "How Tech Has Led the Evolution of Media and a Glimpse at What's to Come." *HuffPost*, May 12, 2015. https://www.huffpost.com/entry/how-tech-has-led-the-evol_b_7224152.

Lewis, E. St. Elmo. *Financial Advertising*. New York: Garland Pub, 1985. https://trove.nla.gov.au/version/22406169.

Lincoln, John. "Considering Amazon Fulfillment Options? Here Is How To Decide." *Inc.com*, July 26, 2017. https://www.inc.com/john-lincoln/how-to-select-the-right-amazon-fulfillment-option-.html.

"Listen to The Big Ticket with Marc Malkin | Podcasts | IHeartRadio." Accessed December 6, 2019. https://www.iheart.com/podcast/28955447/.

Lister, Mary. "37 Staggering Video Marketing Statistics for 2018." *WordStream*, June 9, 2019. https://www.wordstream.com/blog/ws/2017/03/08/video-marketing-statistics.

Lowes. "Are You Still Shopping for Paint?," December 25, 2016.

Madrigal, Alexis C. "The Fall of Facebook." *The Atlantic*, November 17, 2014. https://www.theatlantic.com/magazine/archive/2014/12/the-fall-of-facebook/382247/.

Manjoo, Farhad. "On Russian Meddling, Mark Zuckerberg Follows a Familiar Playbook." *The New York Times*, September 22, 2017, sec. Technology. https://www.nytimes.com/2017/09/22/technology/mark-zuckerberg-facebook-russian-ads.html.

Manson, Marshall. "Facebook Zero: Considering Life After the Demise of Organic Reach." *Ogilvy Greece,* March 17, 2014. https://ogilvy.gr/feed/facebook-zero-considering-life-after-the-demise-of-organic-reach.

Martineau, Paris, and Louise Matsakis. "Why It's Hard to Escape Amazon's Long Reach." *Wired*, December 23, 2018. https://www.wired.com/story/why-hard-escape-amazons-long-reach/.

McAlone, Nathan. "Teens Watch More Netflix and YouTube than TV - Business Insider." *Business Insider*, May 1, 2017. https://www.businessinsider.com/teens-watching-netflix-youtube-more-than-tv-2017-5.

Mckew, Molly. "Did Russia Affect the 2016 Election? It's Now Undeniable." *Wired*, February 16, 2018. https://www.wired.com/story/did-russia-affect-the-2016-election-its-now-undeniable/.

McKinsey & Company. "Thinking inside the Subscription Box: New Research on e-Commerce Consumers," February 2018. https://www.mckinsey.com/industries/technology-media-and-telecommunications/our-insights/thinking-inside-the-subscription-box-new-research-on-ecommerce-consumers.

McLuhan, Marshall, and Quentin Fiore. *The Medium Is the Massage*. 1 edition. Berkeley, CA: Ginko Press, 2001.

Mercer, Greg. "Amazon PPC Ultimate Guide: How to Advertise Your Products 2018." *Jungle Scout*: Amazon Product Research Made Easy, March 22, 2018. https://www.junglescout.com/blog/amazon-ppc-guide-2018/.

Michael, Mark. "The Modern Consumer Decision-Making Journey." Mark Michael. Accessed December 6, 2019. https://www.markmichael.io/insights/the-modern-consumer-customer-decision-making-journey.

Modena, Jane. "Google Shopping Campaigns Guide: Best Practices, Tips &

Tricks." *WordStream*, September 18, 2019. https://www.wordstream.com/blog/ws/2015/03/04/google-shopping-campaigns-tips-tricks.

Morris, Ian. "Netflix Is Now Bigger Than Cable TV." *Forbes*, June 13, 2017. https://www.forbes.com/sites/ianmorris/2017/06/13/netflix-is-now-bigger-than-cable-tv/#765a61da158b.

Mueller III, Robert S. "Report on the Investigation into Russian Interference in the 2016 Presidential Election." Washington, D.C: DOJ, 2019. https://www.justice.gov/storage/report.pdf.

Mull, Amanda. "There Is Too Much Stuff." *The Atlantic*, May 24, 2019. https://www.theatlantic.com/health/archive/2019/05/too-many-options/590185/.

Murphy, Mike. "Apple's 'Walled Garden' Approach to Content Has Paid off Massively." *Quartz*, August 3, 2017. https://qz.com/1045671/apples-walled-garden-approach-to-apps-and-music-has-paid-off-massively-aapl/.

———. "You Might Not Have Heard of Fanatics yet—but It's Taking over Sports Apparel One League at a Time." *Quartz*, April 25, 2019. https://qz.com/1600107/fanatics-has-found-a-way-to-make-itself-effectively-amazon-proof/.

Nagaraj, Ankitha. "A Beginners Guide to Amazon Product Display Ads With Benefits." *Amazon Seller Blog* - Seller Updates & Strategies, August 1, 2018. https://www.sellerapp.com/blog/amazon-product-display-ads/.

National Association for College Admission Counseling. "2017 STATE OF COLLEGE ADMISSION." *Nacacnet.org*, n.d. https://www.nacacnet.org/globalassets/documents/publications/research/soca17_ch1.pdf.

Nickinson, Phil, Alex Dobie, and Jerry Hildenbrand. "How Nexus, Samsung, and Apple Drove Android's Evolution." *Android Central*, November 4, 2015. https://www.androidcentral.com/android-makes-it-big.

Nieva, Richard. "Google Maps Has Now Photographed 10 Million Miles in Street View - CNET." *CNET*, December 13, 2019. https://www.cnet.com/news/google-maps-has-now-photographed-10-million-miles-in-street-view/.

Norton, Steven. "Fanatics Revamps Cloud Platform, Addressing the Online Unpredictability of Sports Fandom." *The Wall Street Journal* (blog), September 17, 2018. https://blogs.wsj.com/cio/2018/09/17/fanatics-revamps-cloud-platform-addressing-the-online-unpredictability-of-sports-fandom/.

Noyes, Katherine. "Google Analytics Just Got a New AI Tool to Help Find Insights Faster." *PCWorld*, September 2, 2016. https://www.pcworld.com/article/3116074/google-analytics-just-got-a-new-ai-tool-to-help-find-insights-faster.html.

O'Beirne, Justin. "Google Maps's Moat." *justinobeirne.com*. Accessed December 5, 2019. https://www.justinobeirne.com/google-maps-moat.

"Our Story | HubSpot - Internet Marketing Company." Accessed December 5, 2019. https://www.hubspot.com/our-story.

Paine, Thomas. *Common Sense: The Origin and Design of Government.* Edited by Coventry House Publishing. Coventry House Publishing, 2016.

Perez, Sarah. "Apple's App Store Revenue Nearly Double That of Google Play in First Half of 2018." *TechCrunch* (blog), July 16, 2018. http://social. techcrunch.com/2018/07/16/apples-app-store-revenue-nearly-double-that-of-google-play-in-first-half-of-2018/.

Peterson, Tim. "Facebook Owns Social Login Scene, But Google's Creeping Up." *AdAge*, January 28, 2016. https://adage.com/article/digital/facebook-owns-social-login-scene-google-s-creeping/302407.

Plummer, Libby. "This Is How Netflix's Top-Secret Recommendation System Works." *Wired UK*, August 22, 2017. https://www.wired.co.uk/article/how-do-netflixs-algorithms-work-machine-learning-helps-to-predict-what-viewers-will-like.

Popular Mechanics. "101 Gadgets That Changed The World," June 15, 2011. https://www.popularmechanics.com/technology/gadgets/reviews/101-gadgets-that-changed-the-world.

Protalinski, Emil. "Facebook Launches Standalone Messenger App for the Web." *VentureBeat* (blog), April 8, 2015. https://venturebeat.com/2015/04/08/facebook-launches-standalone-messenger-app-for-the-web/.

Quigley, Charles. "Constitutional Democracy." *Center for Civic Education.* Accessed December 15, 2019. https://www.civiced.org/resources/publications/resource-materials/390-constitutional-democracy.

Rey, Jason Del. "Yes, Google Punished EBay for Bad SEO Practices, but It Wasn't Part of 'Panda' Update." *Vox*, May 23, 2014. https://www.vox.com/2014/5/23/11627220/yes-google-punished-ebay-for-bad-seo-practices-but-it-wasnt-part-of.

Rheinlander, Scott. "Everything You Wanted to Know About Marketing Attribution Models (but Were Afraid to Ask)." *Salesforce Blog*, April 19, 2019. https://www.salesforce.com/blog/2017/11/what-is-marketing-attribution-model.html.

Richter, Felix. "Amazon Passes 100 Million Prime Members in the U.S." Digital image, January 18, 2019. https://www.statista.com/chart/5232/amazon-prime-members/.

Robert Morse. "Freshmen Students Say Rankings Aren't Key Factor in College Choice." *US News*, January 31, 2013. https://www.usnews.com/

education/blogs/college-rankings-blog/2013/01/31/freshmen-students-say-rankings-arent-key-factor-in-college-choice.

Rosen, Guy, Katie Harbath, Nathaniel Gleicher, and Rob Leathern. "Helping to Protect the 2020 US Elections." *Facebook Newsroom* (blog), October 21, 2019. https://about.fb.com/news/2019/10/update-on-election-integrity-efforts/.

Rosenberg, Matthew, Nicholas Confessore, and Carole Cadwalladr. "How Trump Consultants Exploited the Facebook Data of Millions." *The New York Times*, March 17, 2018, sec. U.S. https://www.nytimes.com/2018/03/17/us/politics/cambridge-analytica-trump-campaign.html.

Rouse, Margaret. "What Is Red Teaming? - Definition from WhatIs.Com." TechTarget | WhatIs.com. Accessed December 6, 2019. https://whatis.techtarget.com/definition/red-teaming.

Salkever, Alex. "Amazon Has a Massive New Division—and No One's Paying Attention to It." *Fortune*, October 8, 2018. https://fortune.com/2018/10/08/amazon-advertising-business-platform/.

Samuelson, Kristen. "3 Benefits to Using Facebook's Value-Based Lookalikes." *AdWeek*, September 12, 2018. https://www.adweek.com/digital/3-benefits-to-using-facebooks-value-based-lookalikes/.

ScrapeHero. "How Many Products Does Amazon Sell? – April 2019," April 24, 2019. https://www.scrapehero.com/number-of-products-on-amazon-april-2019/.

Schaefer, Mark. "Content Shock: Why Content Marketing Is Not a Sustainable Strategy." *Schaefer Marketing Solutions*: We Help Businesses {grow}, January 6, 2014. https://businessesgrow.com/2014/01/06/content-shock/.

StatCounter Global Stats. "Search Engine Market Share Worldwide," January 15, 2019. https://gs.statcounter.com/search-engine-market-share.

Senate Select Committee on Intelligence. "Russian Active Measures Campaigns and Interference in 2016 U.S. Election: Volume 1." 116th Cong. § 1, 2019. https://www.intelligence.senate.gov/sites/default/files/documents/Report_Volume1.pdf.

———. "Russian Active Measures Campaigns and Interference in 2016 U.S. Election: Volume 2." 116th Cong. § 1, 2019. https://www.intelligence.senate.gov/sites/default/files/documents/Report_Volume2.pdf.

SEO Book. "How Does Google Rank Websites & Other Content in Their Search Results?" Accessed December 5, 2019. http://www.seobook.com/learn-seo/infographics/how-search-works.php.

Serra, Richard, and Clara Weyergraf. *Richard Serra: Interviews, Etc. 1970-1980*.

Place of publication not identified: Archer Fields Pr, 1981.

Shatzkin, Mike. "A Changing Book Business: It All Seems to Be Flowing Downhill to Amazon." *The Idea Logical Company*, January 22, 2018. https://www.idealog.com/blog/changing-book-business-seems-flowing-downhill-amazon/.

Shelley, Percy Bysshe. *Shelley's Poetry and Prose: Authoritative Texts, Criticism*. Edited by Donald H. Reiman and Sharon B. Powers. 1st edition. New York: W W Norton & Co Inc, 1977.

Shih, Joseph. "AdWords: Google Search Partners List 2019." *Twinword, Inc.* (blog), January 5, 2019. https://www.twinword.com/blog/adwords-google-search-partners-list/.

Silver, Nate. "How Much Did Russian Interference Affect The 2016 Election?" *FiveThirtyEight* (blog), February 16, 2018. https://fivethirtyeight.com/features/how-much-did-russian-interference-affect-the-2016-election/.

Smith, Brad. "Google Ads Keyword Planner: What Has Changed (And How To Use It)." *AdEspresso* (blog), June 17, 2019. https://adespresso.com/blog/google-keyword-planner/.

Smulyan, Susan. *Selling Radio: The Commercialization of American Broadcasting, 1920-1934*. Washington: Smithsonian Institution Press, 1994.

StackShare. "Bing Maps API vs Google Maps vs Mapbox | What Are the Differences?," February 7, 2019. https://stackshare.io/stackups/bing-maps-api-vs-google-maps-vs-mapbox.

Steinberg, S. H. *Five Hundred Years of Printing*. 3rd ed. Harmondsworth: Penguin Books, 1974.

Stokes, Richard. "I Left the Ad Industry Because Our Use of Data Tracking Terrified Me." *Fast Company*, June 6, 2019. https://www.fastcompany.com/90359992/an-ad-tech-pioneer-on-where-our-data-economy-went-wrong-and-how-to-fix-it.

Stone, Brad. *The Everything Store: Jeff Bezos and the Age of Amazon*. Reprint edition. New York, NY: Back Bay Books, 2014.

Study Lib. "Blockbuster Rewards Membership Guide," February 8, 2002. https://studylib.net/doc/8877514/blockbuster-rewards-membership-guide.

Sullivan, Danny. "Post-PRISM, Google Confirms Quietly Moving To Make All Searches Secure, Except For Ad Clicks." *Search Engine Land*, September 23, 2013. https://searchengineland.com/post-prism-google-secure-searches-172487.

Sullivan, Mark. "Apple Gets All Moody in New Privacy Ad for World Series." *Fast Company*, October 25, 2019. https://www.fastcompany.com/90422794/apple-gets-all-moody-in-new-privacy-ad-for-world-series.

Taparia, Neal. "5 Things You Can Learn About 'Growth Hacking' From The Man Who Coined The Term." *Forbes*, July 22, 2014. https://www. forbes.com/sites/nealtaparia/2014/07/22/5-things-i-learned-about-growth-hacking-from-the-man-who-coined-the-term/.

Taylor, Glenn. "Fanatics Scores 27,000 Personalized Marketing Campaigns With Salesforce." *Retail TouchPoints*, August 29, 2016. https://www. retailtouchpoints.com/features/retail-success-stories/fanatics-scores-27-000-personalized-marketing-campaigns-with-salesforce.

"The World's Most Valuable Resource Is No Longer Oil, but Data." *The Economist*, May 6, 2017. https://www.economist.com/leaders/2017/05/06/the-worlds-most-valuable-resource-is-no-longer-oil-but-data.

Thompson, Ben. "Data Factories." *Stratechery*, October 2, 2018. https:// stratechery.com/2018/data-factories/.

———. "Messaging: Mobile's Killer App." *Stratechery*, February 18, 2014. https://stratechery.com/2014/messaging-mobiles-killer-app/.

Thompson, Derek. "The Print Apocalypse of American Newspapers." *The Atlantic*, November 3, 2016. https://www.theatlantic.com/business/archive/2016/11/the-print-apocalypse-and-how-to-survive-it/506429/.

Thompson, Nicholas, and Fred Vogelstein. "15 Months of Fresh Hell Inside Facebook." *Wired*, April 16, 2019. https://www.wired.com/story/facebook-mark-zuckerberg-15-months-of-fresh-hell/.

Vlahos, James. *Talk to Me: How Voice Computing Will Transform the Way We Live, Work, and Think*. Boston, New York: Eamon Dolan/Houghton Mifflin Harcourt, 2019.

Walker, Ben. "Every Day Big Data Statistics – 2.5 Quintillion Bytes of Data Created Daily." *VCloud News* (blog), April 5, 2015. http://www.vcloudnews.com/every-day-big-data-statistics-2-5-quintillion-bytes-of-data-created-daily/.

Ward, Jacob. "Data, Not Privacy, Is the Real Danger." *NBC News*, February 4, 2019. https://www.nbcnews.com/business/business-news/why-data-not-privacy-real-danger-n966621.

Ward, Matt. "Product to Platform — Inside Amazon's Dominance." *Medium*, August 26, 2018. https://becominghuman.ai/product-to-platform-inside-amazons-dominance-8d051a24d2c2.

———. "Why Is Amazon the Most Powerful Platform in the World?" *Better Marketing*, April 18, 2018. https://medium.com/better-marketing/product-to-platform-inside-amazons-dominance-bacef9e80585.

Warzel, Charlie. "Facebook Isn't Sorry — It Just Wants Your Data." *BuzzFeed News*, October 9, 2018. https://www.buzzfeednews.com/article/

charliewarzel/facebook-isnt-sorry-it-just-wants-your-data.

We Are Social. "Percentage of All Global Web Pages Served to Mobile Phones from 2009 to 2018." *Chart. Statista*, January 29, 2018. https://www.statista.com/statistics/241462/global-mobile-phone-website-traffic-share/.

———. "Und Hootsuite, Und DataReportal. "Most Popular Global Mobile Messenger Apps as of October 2019, Based on Number of Monthly Active Users (in Millions)." Chart, October 25, 2019. https://www.statista.com/statistics/258749/most-popular-global-mobile-messenger-apps/.

"WeChat's World, WeChat's World." *The Economist*, August 6, 2016. https://www.economist.com/business/2016/08/06/wechats-world.

WhatsApp. "About WhatsApp." Accessed December 5, 2019. https://www.whatsapp.com/about/.

White, Rebecca. "The Ultimate Guide to Amazon Advertising," October 22, 2019. https://blog.hubspot.com/marketing/amazon-advertising.

Wilke, Jeffrey. *Virtuous Cycle*. Accessed December 6, 2019. https://www.youtube.com/watch?v=5jcDlGn-tZA.

Wilson, Jen. "Make-A-Wish Greater Bay Area: Miles' Wish to Be Batkid." *Make-A-Wish Greater Bay Area*, January 15, 2014. http://sf.wish.org/en/wishes/wish-stories/i-wish-to-be/wish-to-be-batkid?cid=soc-fb-025-000.

Wong, Julia Carrie. "Facebook Overhauls News Feed in Favor of 'Meaningful Social Interactions.'" *The Guardian*, January 12, 2018, sec. Technology. https://www.theguardian.com/technology/2018/jan/11/facebook-news-feed-algorithm-overhaul-mark-zuckerberg.

World Population Review. "China Population 2019 (Demographics, Maps, Graphs)," February 23, 2019. http://worldpopulationreview.com/countries/china-population/.

World Population Review. "India Population 2019 (Demographics, Maps, Graphs)," February 23, 2019. http://worldpopulationreview.com/countries/india-population/.

"WorldWideWebSize.Com | The Size of the World Wide Web (The Internet)." Accessed October 3, 2018. https://www.worldwidewebsize.com/.

Wu, Tim. *The Attention Merchants: The Epic Scramble to Get Inside Our Heads*. First Edition edition. New York: Knopf, 2016.

Yeung, Ken. "Facebook: 60 Million Businesses Have Pages, 4 Million Actively Advertise." *VentureBeat* (blog), September 27, 2016. https://venturebeat.com/2016/09/27/facebook-60-million-businesses-have-pages-4-million-actively-advertise/.

Young, Miles. *Ogilvy on Advertising in the Digital Age*. London: Goodman

Books, 2017.

Young, Wesley. "Location Based Geo-Targeting Boosts Paid Search Ad Performance...Or Does It?" *Search Engine Land*, February 4, 2015. https:// searchengineland.com/location-based-geo-targeting-boosts-paid-search-ad-performance-importance-truly-local-data-search-marketing-decisions-213765.

Zaczkiewicz, Arthur. "Study Reveals Amazon at 'Center' of Customer Shopping Journey." *Yahoo! Lifestyle*, May 19, 2019. https://www.yahoo.com/ lifestyle/study-reveals-amazon-center-customer-212502954.html.

Zak, Annie. "Alaska's Last 2 Blockbuster Stores Are Closing, Leaving Just One in the U.S." *Anchorage Daily News*, July 13, 2018. https://www.adn. com/business-economy/2018/07/12/the-last-two-blockbuster-stores-in-alaska-are-set-to-close/.

ABOUT THE AUTHOR

Jon Hinderliter is the Director of Marketing and Communications for University College at Washington University in St. Louis, where he manages integrated marketing strategies to help adult learners experience the impact of earning a world-class education. With over a decade of experience in data-driven marketing, he has managed hundreds of digital marketing campaigns, websites, social media properties, and mobile apps. He has a master's from Southern Illinois University Edwardsville where he wrote about the impact of fake blogs in 2010 and predicted the possibility of foreign influence on social media. Jon is a veteran, who retired in 2018 after 20 years from the U.S. Coast Guard Reserve with four years of active duty service after 9/11.

ABOUT THE PUBLISHER
TACTICAL 16

Tactical 16 Publishing is an unconventional publisher that understands the therapeutic value inherent in writing. We help veterans, first responders, and their families and friends to tell their stories using their words.

We are on a mission to capture the history of America's heroes: stories about sacrifices during chaos, humor amid tragedy, and victories learned from experiences not readily recreated—real stories from real people.

Tactical 16 has published books in leadership, business, fiction, and children's genres. We produce all types of works, from self-help to memoirs that preserve unique stories not yet told.

You don't have to be a polished author to join our ranks. If you can write with passion and be unapologetic, we want to talk. Go to Tactical16.com to contact us and to learn more.